OUT OF THE MAZE

OUT OF THE MAZE

Noel Davidson

AMBASSADOR

Belfast Northern Ireland Greenville South Carolina

Out of the Maze
© Copyright 2000 Noel Davidson

ISBN 1   84030 090 6

Ambassador Publications
a division of
Ambassador Productions Ltd.
Providence House
Ardenlee Street,
Belfast,
BT6 8QJ
Northern Ireland
www.ambassador-productions.com

Emerald House
427 Wade Hampton Blvd.
Greenville
SC 29609, USA
www.emeraldhouse.com

CONTENTS

INTRODUCTION

His face was a picture as he read the article.

I had just handed him the morning newspaper, and the man-in-my-study sat silently, his eyes scanning down the lines.

There were occasional short sharp smiles of recognition interspersed by an occasional creasing of the brows, betraying brief bewilderment.

When he had finished reading the article describing a number of former inmates who had graduated from The Maze prison, that 'university of terror' with big ideas and subsequently even bigger salaries, Thomas Martin handed me back my paper with a warm grin and a resigned nod of the head.

"They have obviously never heard about me!" he observed, with a laugh.

And obviously neither they had!

I looked across at where he sat. A short but not stout, squat but not fat, once-upon-a-time hard-wee-nut. This man had served more than six years in The Maze for relatively minor offences. Some of the prisoners who were due to be released later that day in July, 2000, had been convicted of multiple murders and had been given multiple life sentences. Yet Thomas seemed to bear no grudge.

"You will probably think this crazy," he went on to remark, pensively, "but I believe that The Maze was part of God's plan for my life...'

Then he broke off. "Pass me back that paper again a minute, Noel," he demanded rather than asked, with the urgency of someone who has just remembered something vitally important.

Glancing down the paper, when it had been returned to him, Thomas soon spotted the particular paragraph which had impressed him enough to request a recall.

"It's true, you know, what it says here," he said. "Listen to this..."

Then he began to read aloud, 'Indeed former paramilitary inmates, loyalist and republican, say The Maze was a vital learning process for young prisoners.'

Folding the paper and setting it down beside him he went on to observe, with the air of one who has 'been-there-done-that', "A lot depends, I suppose, on what it is that you learn!"

That was true, too.

For it was what Thomas Martin had learnt in prison that had changed his life.

It was in that prison, and on the protest, after a difficult childhood and a turbulent teenage culminating in paramilitary involvement, that he learnt life's most important lesson.

It was that he, a sinner, needed a Saviour, and that Jesus, Who had died to pay the penalty for all his sins, was willing to enter and both change and control his life.

That, though by far the most important and impactive, was not his only Maze discovery.

Thomas soon found out what it was like to live for his new Commander in that far-from-sympathetic environment.

He was called upon to endure taunts, ranging in intensity from gentle gibes to relentless ridicule.

He learnt what it meant to stand up and be counted on legs that could barely stand up at all.

And he was eventually enabled, through it all, to provide practical, personal proof of the preserving power of God.

It was when in The Maze, too, that he was to find out that in addition to a God of love in heaven, there were also two people on earth who loved him dearly. One was his father, who had supported him faithfully through many hardships during his prison term, and the other was a shy girl from Upper Ballinderry...But therein lies another story. A love story within a life story...

When Thomas was released from The Maze, early in 1988, a saved man, and a free man, another voyage of discovery began. There was so much he still had to learn about God's plans to provide for him. His girl-friend was soon to become his wife and they were to have three sons, the most recent of whom, Timothy, was born just a few weeks ago. And what could a converted paramilitary prisoner do for the rest of his days?...

When researching this book recently, a Christian who ministered to many of the inmates in Northern Ireland's prisons during their busiest days all through the darkest days of our 'Troubles', remarked emphatically, "Thomas Martin was one of the best things to come out of the Maze."

It will be interesting, when you read this book, to see if you agree with her.

I do.

Noel I. Davidson,
August, 2000.

1

GOING BACK, OVER THERE

"I am taking you back to Northern Ireland, boys," Tommy Martin explained to his three sons, Colin, Thomas and David one evening. "Your mother and I haven't been getting on too well lately, and I am going back to live with my mother, your granny, and her new husband, outside a place called Lurgan, over there."

To his seven-year-old son Thomas, the fact that his parents were splitting up came as no surprise. Although they had both come from Northern Ireland, and were now living in Nottingham, England, where father had been serving in the Army, Thomas knew in his childish mind that things weren't quite right in his home.

When his parents were both together in the house there were constant vicious arguments. Cruel nasty things were said. And shouted.

He didn't like it, but had become used to it. It was part and parcel of his life.

Although things hadn't always been entirely blissful at home young Thomas had mixed feelings at the prospect of going to Northern Ireland. To live 'over there'.

His father had said he was 'going back' to the province, but for Thomas and his older brother Colin and younger brother David it would be their first experience of their parents' homeland. They had heard both father and mother speak of it. At different times. And in different tones. Sometimes in glowing terms. And sometimes not quite so. It all seemed to depend on the mood of the moment.

So Thomas wasn't quite sure just what to expect.

The picture his father painted that evening, though, proved enough to convince him that it would all work out for the best.

A farm near Lough Neagh, with all the freedom of rural life. Fields and hedges. Byres and barns. Cows and calves. Dogs and pups. Cats and kittens. Pigs and poultry. Hens and eggs. And fresh clean air. A clear blue sky over all...

It would certainly be a change from Nottingham.

And hopefully a change for the better.

Whether he liked it or not though, Thomas knew that he had no choice in the matter. He and his brothers were going. They had to. No question. That was it.

Crossing the Irish Sea to Belfast on 'the Liverpool boat' promised to be an exciting experience for the three brothers. They had seen small boats and barges on the rivers and canals of England, but none of them was anything like this! And they were actually going on it!

The thrill of their overnight over-the-sea trip was rather tempered for the young adventurers when their father found a few seats in the lounge and saw them settled down. Curled up in their coats.

"You three boys must go to sleep in your seats there," he told them, looking very stern, "or the captain will throw you off this boat. So get to sleep as soon as you can, and don't move from where you are. I have some things to do but I will come back for you in the morning before it is time to go ashore."

Father hadn't really some things to do. He only had one thing to do. That was go to the bar and drink. And drink. And drink.

For Tommy Martin had begun to spend more and more of his money and more and more of his time in bars. And on booze. It was fast becoming an all-consuming craving.

So the night of the trip across from Liverpool to Belfast, which could have been such a memorable experience for three lively, interested boys turned out to be a night of seemingly endless nervous sleeplessness.

The seats, from which they had been solemnly instructed not to move, seemed to become harder somehow as the night ticked slowly by, wakeful minute by wakeful minute.

They found it almost impossible to close an eye for anything more than five minutes with the bustle around them.

There always seemed to be people going somewhere, or doing something.

All through the night.

And the man across from them, all wrapped up in the blanket which he must have brought with him just snored, and snored, and snored. In fifty different sharps and flats.

All through the night.

The throb of the engines, though, was the worst thing of all.

Every time Thomas rested his head on the side of the seat, or the back of the seat, the throb, throb, throb of the engines went bang, bang, bang in his brain.

All through the night.

How could he sleep? How could anybody sleep?

Anyway he had to keep half an eye open for the captain. For if Thomas saw a man in a uniform coming near him he needed to be ready to pretend to be asleep.

For he wouldn't like to be thrown off that boat, into the sea.

That must be awful!

The journey was completed safely, however, and Tommy Martin took his three sons to live with their grandparents, as he had promised. And there began one of the happiest years in an otherwise bleak childhood for Thomas and his two brothers.

Granny and 'granda' Dougan lived on a farm at Ardmore, near Lurgan, in County Armagh. It was, as their father had told them, a working farm near Lough Neagh. Perhaps it was not quite the idyllic place he had described in his that's-where-we-are-going-to-boys introductory speech but it was a busy family farm, with lots to do and see.

In late August, the three brothers were enrolled at Ardmore Primary School, and discovered, to their initial dismay, that they would have to walk there and back. It was a mile each way. Every day.

To prepare them for the tramp-to-school in the approaching autumn and winter days, Tommy Martin, encouraged by granny no doubt, made one of his few major purchases for his sons. He took all three of them into Lurgan one day and bought them each a pair of hob-nail boots.

"Those will be great boots for the winter day," he assured his not-so-sure sons on the way home. "They will protect your feet against the cold and damp."

Perhaps they would. And perhaps they did. But Thomas didn't like his boots. For when Colin, David and he set out for school in the morning he was afraid that the neighbours would think that the Army had come into the district to prepare for a long march. Instead of that it was just three young lads on the daily trudge to school.

Although he didn't like the boots for their weight and the clump-clump here-we-come noise they made, Thomas did usually enjoy that walk to school. Especially on cool crisp autumn, new-life spring or sunny summer mornings.

There was just so much to see and do!

The lad who had spent the first seven years of his life in an English city learnt more Environmental Science on the way to school than he ever did in it!

The early morning hand inspection before lessons caused him frequent problems, though. For on the walk to school he often managed to mess up the checked-by-granny-before-he-left-home hands.

On many an autumn morning they were stained purple-black with the juice of some delicious blackberries which had been pulled and eaten because they had looked so tempting, sitting sparkling with sunlit dew. And on spring mornings his hands were often streaked with his own congealed blood from the myriad scratches obtained by poking about in hawthorn hedges looking for birds' nests. Or they occasionally ended up with caked mud under the nails from trying to stop himself when sliding down a bank somewhere.

What a mess they were sometimes!

But when Thomas had been sent outside to wash the offending hands he was admitted to lessons. These he usually found tolerable. Enjoyable even, every now and then. He always kept an eye on the window, though. To keep a check on the weather for the homeward trip. Which often took even longer that the schoolward one!

That was a wonderful year!

Thomas loved his grandparents who were so very kind, and the pace of the countryside, which was so very peaceful.

Although he had always hoped that they could stay there for ever, young Thomas knew that it was an impossible dream. They couldn't. Something was bound to happen to burst the bubble. And it did.

It was father who had further news for his three boys the next summer.

"I am renting a place in Lurgan for us to move into in August, boys," he informed them one day in late June. "You are all having a great time here, I know, but it is just too much for your granny. She just can't cope with us all any more."

It was sad, but true.

Granny and granda were finding the caring and catering for their four guests an increasing strain. With Tommy and his three spirited sons around the house there was hardly ever a quiet room to sit in. Or even a free chair to sit on. And that not to mention all the additional cooking and cleaning, and washing and ironing, which had to be done, almost daily.

It was the only sensible solution.

They would have to move out.

To 'a place in Lurgan. In August.'

2

HAPPY CHRISTMAS

A place in Lurgan.

And what a place it turned out to be!

34 James Street was an almost derelict house in a street of mostly derelict houses. When Tommy Martin moved his three sons into their new abode they didn't have any neighbours. They couldn't have. For the houses on either side of them had been wrecked and vandalized long before. But since number 34 had both glass in the windows and a front door that closed it was deemed habitable, and so became home for the four Martins.

The house could possibly have been fixed up to an acceptable standard of repair, and touched up to a pleasing standard of decor, if anyone had shown any interest in it.

Unfortunately, though, nobody did.

Father had only one interest. His obsession with alcohol had become even worse now that he had escaped from his mother's caring and controlling clutches.

And the boys, too, had only one interest. But theirs was different. For theirs was an interest which was soon to become their prime concern.

It was staying alive. The need to survive.

Their main task each day was to live through that day. And then face tomorrow. After that they had to struggle through next week.

They didn't even dare to count time in months. Or years. That would be totally out of the question.

What a change, then, life in Lurgan proved to be from life by Lough Neagh!

The three lads were sent to Carrick Primary School in the town, a big school with big classes. It was so far removed from the more intimate personal atmosphere of Ardmore.

They were left alone a lot, too. Left to their own devices for hours, even days, at a time.

What happened was that one or some of their father's cronies would call at the door and ask, "Are you coming down to the pub for the darts match, Tommy?"

And Tommy, who was always ready to go down to the pub for anything, almost always went, leaving his three sons to fend for themselves.

If the weeknights were bad, the weekends were often worse. There were times when father disappeared on a Friday night and didn't reappear in 34 James Street until the Sunday night. Or even Monday morning.

Colin, Thomas and David spent many nights roaming the streets of Lurgan until late at night. They stayed out until they were both tired and cold. Then the crept back home and crawled into bed. Still both tired and cold.

It was a far cry from the warmth and care of granny's home in Ardmore.

When it appeared that they were down as far as they could go, and that things couldn't possibly get any worse for Thomas and his two brothers, they did.

It all began one night when father decided to invite some of his pals-from-the-pub home for a game of cards after closing time. Eleven-thirty perhaps. This had happened a few times before, so the boys knew what to expect. They were told to, "Go on up to bed and don't dare come down for anything!" Tempers had flared on previous occasions, and voices had been raised, but never before had events taken the particularly nasty turn that they did on that particular night.

Thomas, lying awake in the bedroom directly above the cramped, crowded, and he was sure smoke-filled, living-room, was following the progress of the game. Or games.

It all sounded so familiar. The chink of glasses. The jingling of money. The short sharp shouts of triumph. The long deep groans in the despair of defeat. The constant disagreements couched in very colourful language...

Suddenly, about half-past one in the morning, when Thomas had just begun to feel drowsy, he was startled wide awake again.

It had all turned ugly down below.

The arguments had become angry.

The swearing became violent and venomous.

Soon the men downstairs, who were all hopelessly inebriated, were bawling at each other uncontrollably.

Then came the sound of chairs falling back onto the floor. Some of card players had staggered to their feet. Fists began to fly. Punches thudded into heads and bodies.

There was a crashing and a smashing sound.

Thomas knew only too well what that meant.

The crashing sound was the table being upended.

The smashing sound was the glasses breaking when they hit the floor.

Mayhem ensued.

The three brothers lay in bed, curled up for heat, starving with hunger, and paralyzed by fear, as their living-room below was systematically wrecked.

The drunken protagonists had begun to throw what furniture they could lift and swing in such a confined space, at each other. Within the space of five minutes their two faded pictures ended up in fragments on the floor.

Then there came the final shattering sound.

It was the front window. The feature which had made their house stand out from all the rest. Now it was gone too. The back of a chair had been shoved out through it and the glass lay smashed to shiny splinters in the street.

With the front window gone, number 34 just looked like number 32 and number 36 and all the other houses in the street. A neglected, derelict building.

One day Thomas was sitting on one of their crudely-repaired chairs, gazing out into the street when he was aware that a shadow had appeared across the window-hole.

It was a woman gazing in!

"Are you looking for something, missus?" Thomas enquired of her, none too graciously.

"Oh sorry, son! I didn't know there was anybody in there!" the lady exclaimed, flabbergasted, then hurried away.

She had thought the house was empty!

The three brothers found life tough.

They had no windows in the downstairs of their house. And no heat anywhere in it. Father spent almost every spare penny he had on drink. He seldom bought clothes for his sons, and he only bought food at the weekend. Provided, of course, that he just happened to be at home at the weekend. If he was out on a binge no food was bought. So the family were left to exist on what had been left over from the previous week.

The boys survived by eating sugar. Out of the packet. In spoonfuls.

And if they could persuade their father to give them a few pence during the week to buy a loaf then they made themselves a special treat. Tomato sauce sandwiches. No butter or margarine or anything fancy like that. Just tomato sauce in sandwiches.

Christmas 1971, when Thomas was ten years old, promised to be a decidedly dismal time for the three intrepid survivors.

They had roamed the streets until late on Christmas Eve, gazing longingly into brightly-lit, gaily-decorated toy-shop windows. They had heard the carols at the Christmas tree, too. Well-dressed, well-fed people singing lustily about 'joy to the world'.

But they were neither well-dressed nor well-fed.

They were poorly dressed and ill-fed.

And 'joy to the world' wasn't something they knew a lot about either.

On Christmas morning they were downstairs, all three of them and father was still upstairs. And still in bed. Sleeping off the night before. They didn't expect to see much of him that day.

Then, in mid-morning they received a most pleasant surprise. It came when two men from the Lurgan Lions Club arrived in their street, knocked on their door, and when Colin went to answer, handed them in a 'Christmas parcel'!

And the Christmas parcel was a Christmas FOOD parcel!

When the three boys spread the contents of that most generous gift out on the floor they could hardly believe it.

All that food! And all for them!

Colin, who was the oldest of them, and the pack leader, surveyed the spoils with an envious eye and a starving stomach and declared, emphatically, "We had better get stuck into all this stuff, boys, before our da wakes up!"

It was wise counsel, and it inspired instant action!

Thomas and David didn't need to be told twice!

What a feast!

Between the three of them they scoffed the lot. They dined with more fervour than finesse, perhaps, but they were very hungry, and this was lovely food.

They ate the jelly cubes straight out of the packet.

They drank the cordial, undiluted, straight out of the bottle.

They broke the Christmas cake up into chunks and ate it out of their hands.

They found themselves spoons and a tin-opener and supped the custard, the pears and the fruit cocktail straight out of their tins.

Oh what a happy, happy Christmas, after all!

3

THE BONFIRE BUILDERS

With no mother in the home, a father who was seldom at home, and seldom sober even when he was, the Martin boys became a law unto themselves.

As they one by one approached their teenage years the three lads spent most of their time roaming the streets. And joining with others, in a 'gang', to protect their territory.

James Street, Lurgan, was close to some predominantly Roman Catholic areas of the town and Thomas and his brothers began to believe that it was their 'loyalist' duty to make sure that no 'nationalist' youth was permitted to linger in their locality.

During the summer months there was hardly a weekend when there wasn't a riot, provoked first by one side, then the other. Nobody worried too much about who had started it, for when a riot was in progress, everybody joined in.

Bottles and bricks, and sticks and stones, were hurled.

Streams of stinging insults freely flowed.

Everything, and anything, flew.

The annual eleventh-of-July-night bonfire was a constant source of aggro. From about March. The 'loyalist' youths of the area considered it their bounden duty, 'For God and Ulster', to collect old tyres, old furniture, and all kinds of combustible rubbish and pile it high. The higher the better. It was always a challenge to have the biggest bonfire in the town.

This ritual took about three months, or more.

Then when it came to about midnight on 'the eleventh night' they set fire to the whole thing and flames licked skywards. To celebrate the arrival of 'The Twelfth'. The day when all the Orangeman marched. To commemorate their 'cultural heritage'.

This fire burned fiercely for three hours, or less.

And then smouldered stubbornly for three days, at least.

Two other very distinctively different groups of youths considered it their bounden duty to thwart the successful building of the James Street bonfire.

The first of these groups was from their 'own side'. 'Loyalist' youths from other areas of the town, short of material, and anxious to have the town's biggest bonfire, would sneak into their area and steal their 'stuff'. Or set it alight where it stood stacked up. Or lay strewn around.

The other group was from 'the other side'. Nationalist youths, who claimed that the building and burning of a bonfire was both 'provocative' and 'triumphalist', would sneak into their area, and steal their 'stuff'. Or set it alight where it stood stacked up. Or lay strewn around.

There were constant bitter battles about bonfires.

The Martin boys, who never had anybody sitting up waiting for them to come home in the evenings, often didn't go home. They camped out! Beside the bonfire. And when it was built, often IN it! To protect it. To prevent a rival gang from either side from setting it alight too soon.

The annual bonfire was a big thing in the life of Thomas Martin.

And it was when collecting for the bonfire with his two brothers and several other teenagers that something happened which had a profound effect on the thirteen year old lad.

It was 7th July, 1975.

During that sultry summer afternoon the bonfire builders were struggling back to their bonfire site carrying or dragging all sorts, shapes and sizes of bonfire fuel when there was a tremendous bang. A mighty explosion.

The ground and everything on it seemed to shake uncontrollably.

Then when the rumble of the explosion had died away there was weird, unnatural stillness. It was uncanny.

The rubbish-collecting bonfire builders were momentarily rooted to the spot, mesmerized.

Suddenly someone shattered the strange silence. "That's up at Carrick School!" he yelled.

What happened next was amazing.

Simultaneously, and as though it had been rehearsed for weeks, every single one of those young people started off at a sprint. Any observer could have been excused for thinking that the starter's gun had just been fired at the Civic Sports! Two tree branches, a chest of drawers without its drawers, and an old mattress with the stuffing sticking out of it here and there, were immediately and instinctively abandoned. They would be picked up on the way back. Perhaps.

Thomas and his friends knew their way about that district. It was their 'home patch' and they could take all 'the short cuts'. And so by a combination of breathless non-stop running, clambering over walls and diving through fences, they were first to arrive at the scene of the explosion. As they panted up to what remained of the front of the School, the sirens of ambulances, fire-appliances and police vehicles could be heard in the distance, but up until that moment none of them had arrived at the bomb site.

What a scene of horror and devastation!

A section of the front of the school around the main door had disappeared. Vanished completely. It had been reduced to a heap of rubble.

Bricks, beams and broken glass had been scattered over a wide area.

It was what had happened to the people who had been in there, though, that made the most indelible impression on the mind of Thomas Martin, aged thirteen-and-a-half.

Two policemen had suffered horrendous injuries. Both were lying motionless, covered in their own caked blood from glass-gash lacerations.

They appeared lifeless.

The school caretaker, whom most of those local teenagers knew well, for many of them had in earlier days attended that Primary School, seemed to have one of his legs impaled on a big metal bar.

He was moaning horribly.

Within minutes of Thomas and his bonfire-building buddies arriving at the scene of the explosion the first police vehicle roared up. This was followed closely by a fire-engine. Then came an ambulance.

And it wasn't long either until the temporarily traumatized teenagers were pushed out of the way. Told in no uncertain terms to, 'Get back out onto the road. We have work to do'. They were chased.

Although they obeyed, reluctantly, Thomas and the others remained watching, listening, missing nothing, until the last of the ambulances had gone wailing away and the forensic scientists had arrived to comb the wreckage for vital clues.

Late that evening Thomas and his brothers left the bomb site. It had become colder and there wasn't much left to see.

Although he had left the bomb site, however, the bomb site didn't leave Thomas.

It haunted him, day and night. For weeks. For months.

Its sights, sounds and smells seemed to pervade his every waking moment.

And it stiffened his resolve.

As he grew older and listened to the older lads talk, Thomas came to the conclusion that building bonfires and flinging bricks and bottles were really only child's play.

There must be something else he could do, some training he could undertake, or some organization he could join that would allow him 'to do his bit' for the 'loyalist' cause.

And also help him 'get his own back' on whoever it was that planted that bomb in that school that day.

4

WELL DONE, ELSIE!

In the absence of a mother in the Martin household there was one woman who took a personal interest in, and displayed a caring concern for, Tommy Martin and his growing boys.

This lady, Elsie, worked with Tommy in the Thompson & Rodgers paper factory in Lurgan, and she liked her frank and friendly workmate, but recognized that he had a few problems in his life. The greatest of these, by far, was the daunting task of rearing his three sons single-handed. This full-time undertaking was not tremendously helped by the fact that Tommy often took the easy way out, the escape-route-from-reality, in alcohol.

So Elsie determined to do what she could to support the struggling family. Help them out wherever and whenever possible.

Elsie's Aid came on two fronts. This kind woman was concerned both for the physical and spiritual welfare of Tommy, Colin, Thomas and David.

Her practical contribution to Martin maintenance was greatly appreciated by Tommy and the boys. Not only did she bring down food for them at regular intervals, saying gently, "Here is a wee something I thought you would all like," not ever fully realizing just how much it was liked, but she also helped with the washing and ironing of the few clothes they possessed.

Young Thomas liked that. And he liked Elsie.

Here was somebody who was interested not only in helping to feed them up to keep them feeling well, but also in helping to clean them up, to keep them looking well.

And when Elsie had gained the trust and confidence of the grateful family then she embarked upon the next phase of her caring programme. Part two of her Preserve the Martins Plan.

As she was leaving the house one day, having done the ironing and dusted the house from top to bottom, Elsie stopped on her way to the door and asked the question which had obviously been on her mind for some time.

"Tommy," she began, addressing father in the corner, "would you like to come along to church with me some time?"

"No, not really, Elsie," came Tommy Martin's instant, it seemed almost prepared, reply, "Church isn't quite my thing.."

He paused for a moment, and then, glancing over to where his three sons were clustered around their battered black-and-white television set, he added, "But the boys would LOVE to go!"

'The boys' hadn't realized up until that moment that they 'would LOVE to go' to church, but when their dad said it, they had to believe it. And they had to do it!

Elsie began to call every Sunday morning to take two-thirds of the Martin family to the Parish Church of St. John the Evangelist, in Sloan Street, Lurgan, with her. Only two of the three boys were free to go for although father had postulated his sons' LOVE for church he had underestimated his own love for his Sunday dinner. And since he had never been at all interested in cooking, one of the three lads had to remain behind to prepare it. Every Sunday.

After a few weeks of regular church attendance Thomas discovered a loophole. A way out. A scheme to save him having to go there every week. Or indeed any week, if he could work it right.

He discovered that neither Colin or David liked being left at home alone to cook the Sunday dinner, and he didn't mind the chore at all. So he paid either of them his pocket-money to allow him to take their place in the cook-the-dinner rota.

Colin and David liked the extra shilling or two. And he liked staying at home.

It worked a treat.

Then Elsie had another idea.

She came back with another proposition. To their father.

"Tommy, Thursday night is Boys' Brigade night down at the Church. Would the boys like to go to that?" she wondered.

"Oh yes Elsie. That would be great. The boys would LOVE to go to that!" father volunteered.

So the boys were enrolled in the Boys' Brigade.

Thomas didn't mind the 'B.B.' as much as the Sunday Service, though. At least you didn't have to sit in the one place all the time at it. There were many interesting activities going on around. Always. AND you were permitted to play football. A big bonus!

Then Elsie had another idea.

Encouraged by the fact that the three teenage lads seemed to attend the Boys' Brigade quite happily, she returned to their dad, just a matter of weeks later, with yet another proposition.

"Tommy, they have started a wee Youth Club on a Friday night round in the Church. Would the boys like to go to that?" she wondered.

"Oh yes Elsie. That would be great. The boys would LOVE to go to that!" father suggested.

So Colin, Thomas and David were sent out every Friday night to the Youth Club in the Church. Every Friday night. To say that Thomas LOVED going would have been something of an exaggeration, but he had to confess to the friends he met and made there, that he did at least LIKE it. The reason for his satisfaction with this particular evening out, though, was again more sporting than spiritual. It had more to do with his enjoyment of playing badminton with somebody at the beginning than his endurance of listening to somebody praying briefly at the end.

That was Sunday morning, Thursday night and Friday night all filled up for the Martin boys.

Then Elsie had another idea for them.

And one day, after ironing, she put it to their dad.

"Tommy, Monday night at the Church is Christian Endeavour night. Do you think the boys would like to go to that? They seem to be enjoying the 'B.B.' and the Youth Club. I'm sure they would like the 'C.E.' too."

"Oh yes, Elsie. That sounds good. The boys would LOVE to go to that!" he responded, predictably.

So Colin, Thomas and David were packed off to the Christian Endeavour on a Monday night, as well.

After allowing the lads to settle into yet another association with the Church, and when she had imagined that they had matured a bit more, something else was instigated. Something which, in its turn, further inspired the enterprising Elsie.

She approached the ever-indebted-to-Elsie Tommy Martin one day about it.

"Tommy, the Church has started confirmation classes for anyone interested on a Wednesday night. I think they would be a big help to the boys. Do you think they would want to go?" she asked.

Having appointed himself as spokesman for his sons, their father wasn't really concerned as to whether they would 'want' to go or not. He just knew how they would feel about such beneficial classes!

"Oh yes, Elsie. The boys would LOVE to go to those!" he decreed confidently.

So, whether they LOVED them or not, or whether they proved to be Elsie's 'big help', or not, Thomas Martin and his two brothers began confirmation classes. On a Wednesday evening.

Now they were going out to church every day of the week except Tuesday and Saturday. And Elsie had designs on one of those days, too!

It was a wet, autumn evening when she arrived round at the Martin home with a bag of goodies for Tommy and the boys to enjoy. And a tape-recorder.

The three lads had been watching a TV programme and Elsie waited. It could prove counter-productive to her cause to interrupt, she knew. When the programme was over and the set switched off the boys realized that they had placed Elsie on hold. And began to try to make amends. They asked her how she was and thanked her for the good things she had brought.

Elsie was astute enough to recognize her opportunity. And she seized it.

"Would you boys like to sing for me? Into the tape-recorder?" she enquired. "Then I will play it back to you and you can hear yourselves!"

It sounded as though this could be a bit of fun. An interesting diversion on a wet evening. The boys were familiar with TV, but not tape-recorders. And the chance to hear themselves singing would certainly be something of a novelty. 'A bit of a laugh', to say the least.

After a few preliminary bouts of nervous giggling the three Martin minstrels sang into the tape-recorder. And what they sang was the only song that they all knew, and that was because it just happened to be a 'hit' at that time.

It was 'Paper Roses', which had been popularized by The Osmonds.

When the ever-so-slightly-embarrassed boys heard their rendition of the popular song they were pleased. They knew they would never make it to the Top of the Pops, but they were pleasantly surprised by their own performance.

And little did they know that Elsie was more than pleasantly surprised. Her offer to the lads to 'sing into the tape-recorder' was merely the first rung of another ladder. An initial audition for a singing position.

For she was working on yet another idea.

Later that evening, when father had returned from wherever he had been, and settled himself as comfortably as he could by their feeble fire, Elsie produced her tape-recorder. And her tape-recording.

"I think you might be interested to hear this, Tommy," she announced, looking uncharacteristically proud of herself.

After they had listened to it through twice, with father looking pleasantly puzzled and the boys glowing with a sort of secret sense of satisfaction, Elsie made her move. Unveiled her plan.

"What do you think of that, Tommy?" she wanted to know, all smiles.

"Oh Elsie that's lovely! That's beautiful!" he exclaimed, displaying an unusual deep delight in his sons' hitherto undiscovered abilities in song.

"Yes that's what I thought, too!" Elsie went on, determined to milk the most out of his benevolent mood, "I knew those boys of yours all had lovely voices. So I thought they might like to join the Junior Choir, at the Church. Practices are starting again on Tuesday night for the winter, and I was wondering if the boys would like to go along ?"

Tommy Martin just had his mouth open to declare, "Oh yes, Elsie, the boys would..." when Thomas junior jumped to his feet. To lodge a protest. He wasn't going to join the junior choir, without registering his honest opinion on such matters.

"Oh no, dad, please not the choir! Anything but the choir!" he objected, having a fair idea of what his bonfire-building buddies would say if they heard he had joined the junior choir. "Do you not know what they DO to you in the choir?! They make a sissy out of you! They dress you up like a wee girl in this frilly collar thing and a big long sweeping robe! Oh no! No! No! Please not the choir!"

With his point powerfully presented he sank back down on to his seat again. His head disappeared into his hands. He was in despair at this development.

The other two boys, inspired by their brother's lead, added their own particular protests in support, but that was all to no avail.

Elsie had been so kind to them all that their father couldn't afford to offend her by refusing to volunteer the vocal talents of his teenage sons to the junior choir

So the three reluctant choristers went along, on a Tuesday evening, to the practices. And they were soon fully-fledged gown-clad members of the junior choir.

Now, thanks to Elsie they were out every day of the week, except Saturday at one church activity or another.

On Monday it was the C.E., Tuesday the junior choir, on Wednesday confirmation classes, Thursday the B.B., and Friday night the Youth Club.

Elsie had a genuine care and concern for Tommy Martin and his three sons. And their souls. And she was prepared to put her concern into practice.

Well done Elsie!

5

'BOYS, I HAVE SOMETHING TO TELL YOU!'

Early in 1976, when Thomas Martin was fourteen, the family moved house. They flitted.

It wasn't a big flit, though. Or far.

It wasn't a big flit for they had nothing big to flit. They had nothing much at all to flit, for that matter.

And it wasn't a far flit either, for they only moved down the same street a few houses. From number 34 James Street to number 10.

When people asked Tommy why he was 'going to all the bother of moving just a dozen doors down the street' he told them that there were three reasons why he thought the move 'would be good.'

For one, it was even closer to the Thompson & Rodgers paper factory where he worked. Indeed it was right next door. Good on hangover mornings.

For two, number 10 was bigger.

And for three, it had glass in the windows.

Although this new house had distinct advantages over their old one, the change of residence for Tommy and his three sons didn't alter the pattern of life for any of them. In any way. A new house couldn't give Tommy Martin a new heart.

All he wanted to do with his spare time was go to the pub. And all he wanted to do with his money, which wasn't even spare, was spend it on drink.

Things became worse. Tommy Martin was seldom sober. .And life for the lads had become a grim struggle for survival.

But things were set to change. For God and Elsie were both on his track.

It was in the summer of that same year, 1976, that Elsie reaped the harvest of her unstinted kindness and unending patience. For the Dick Saunders Way To Life Crusade team came and pitched a large tent in the grounds of Lurgan Junior High School and began advertising their meetings throughout the town. Large posters appeared on local hoardings. Announcements were made in local churches.

Then Elsie, who had made Tommy Martin and his family the target of much practical kindness and the subject of much private prayer, asked the hard-working hard-drinking father, if he would like to 'go along to hear Dick Saunders'.

Since she had carefully chosen a strategic moment to ask him, when he was alone, sober, and in a grateful frame of mind, Tommy must not have considered it fair to volunteer to send 'the boys'. Although he had no doubt but that 'they would LOVE to go'!

He gave his fellow-employee and family friend a fairly non-committal answer.

"I will probably go along sometime, Elsie," he told her, trying to put her off.

Elsie was a persistent person though. She had picked up the scent of a soul and she was determined to remain in the hunt. It would take more than one half-hearted reply to put her off!

At every opportunity, whether convenient or contrived, she asked him again. And again. And again.

Finally Tommy Martin could take it no more.

He submitted. Succumbed. Surrendered.

And promised to go. But, 'Just the once, mind you!'

There had been much talk about the Crusade in the town over the previous days. Tommy had heard them talking about people who had gone and had 'got saved'.

But that kind of thing definitely wasn't for him. He was sure God wouldn't have a lot of need of a useless down-and-out drunk like him. The Almighty had plenty of clean-living no-messing ministers and people like that around Him, to do His bidding. What would He want with Tommy 'the wee wino' Martin?

But Elsie had been such a help to them, and if only for the sake of a few more ironed shirts or another tin or two of chocolate biscuits, he would go 'just the once'. Just to please her.

Since he had never mentioned Elsie or her invitations to the family, it came as a surprise to the three lads to see their father 'getting all dressed up' one evening. They had been used to seeing him setting out for the pub in the evening, nearly every evening, in his working clothes. Now here was something completely different.

Colin, Thomas and David exchanged puzzled glances and furtive whispers as their father washed thoroughly after work, and then shaved for the second time in the same day. Following this uncharacteristic grooming session Tommy proceeded to change his shirt into one of the few clean ones he possessed, which was one that the long-suffering Elsie had ironed and left hanging in his thinly-populated wardrobe.

The ultimate bafflement for the three totally mystified teenage observers came, though, when he rummaged through a few drawers and produced a fairly-old-but-looked-like-new-seldom-if-ever-worn tie.

Their dad was going to wear a tie!

A tie!

A tie! Not for a wedding or to a wake. But on just an ordinary weeknight!

What on earth was going on?!

As he passed through the living-room on the way out Colin acted as spokesman, voicing the curiosity of all of them.

"Will we find you down in the Windsor Bar if we need you, da, as usual?" he probed.

"No, I'm not going down to the Windsor tonight, boys," father obviously thought he had better explain. "I am going to a gospel mission in that tent up in the grounds of the Junior High."

With that he closed the front door firmly after him , and stepped out into the street, leaving his sons standing aghast.

Their da at a gospel mission! They weren't quite sure what a 'gospel mission' was, but they were quite sure that it didn't sound like something their father would be heavily into!

It was a summer night though, and the three lively lads had things to do. There were mates to meet and summer streets and leafy lanes to visit and explore.

So the forgot about their father,

'All dolled up' and out at 'a gospel mission'.

They forgot about him, until he came home, much later.

But none of the boys ever forgot what happened then...

It was almost half past ten when Tommy Martin arrived home. His three sons had been in for almost an hour at the time, for the evening outside had turned chilly. Everybody else had gone home 'to watch TV'. So they did too.

Thomas and David were sprawled out in front of the ever-blaring TV set when their father arrived into the living room. Colin, who had been in their tiny kitchen, came and stood uneasily in the doorway between the two rooms.

What would be that night's first blast? they all wondered.

It was usually either, "Turn that thing down a bit!"

Or, "Turn over to the other side! Did you not know I wanted to watch the match?!"

Or, "Make me something to eat somebody! NOW!"

No matter what the boys were doing it was never right. Their father always seemed to find something to complain about. Or something to keep them all on their toes...

But not that night.

That night was different.

Tommy Martin looked round at all three of them in turn, smiling at each before remarking, "I don't think I'll bother with anything to eat tonight, lads. I am a bit tired so I think I will just head on up to bed!"

He then turned on his heel and did just that. He set off up the stairs. To bed!

What has got into the man? his sons wondered.

No shouting. And no supper. Strange.

Twenty minutes later a shout did come, however.

But it wasn't an angry shout.

It wasn't an 'If-you-don't-come-quick-I'll-knock-your-block-off!' kind of shout.

No. This, like the going out to the mission, and the coming home from the mission, was something completely different.

The lads in the living-room heard their dad get out of his bed just above them and come to the top of the stairs and call, all calm and controlled, "Could you all come up here a minute, boys? I have something to tell you!"

Although unsure of what was coming next, on this already peculiar evening, the family knew from past experience that when father called they had to come. It could prove painful to refuse.

So all three of them arrived hesitantly in their father's bedroom, wondering what this singular summons was all about.

They found that their father was back in bed. He was sitting up, his face shining.

"Sit down there somewhere, boys" was his initial greeting to them. He waved his arm welcomingly, but limply, around the small room. He was probably trying to pinpoint 'somewhere'. Which to his invited audience could have been anywhere.

They settled themselves quickly, nonetheless.

Colin and David perched precariously on the edge of the bed, and Thomas folded back the shirt and trousers which had been thrown carelessly across the single bentwood chair in the bedroom. And he perched precariously on the outer five inches of it.

Now the scene was set. For father's big announcement.

And big announcement it was!

Moving his head gently to gaze intently into all three expectant faces as he spoke, Tommy Martin said softly, but ever so sincerely, "Lads, your old man has got saved."

It was now the boys' turn to look from one to the other, then back to their undeniably ever-so-delighted dad, who was sitting up in bed with an air of complete but hitherto unfound fulfilment. He had the appearance of someone who had just swum the English Channel or climbed Mount Everest. Without even getting out of bed.

His face was a picture of peace.

The boys were bewildered. They were at a complete loss to know what to think, never mind **say**, in the situation.

Whatever this being 'saved' meant it certainly seemed to have pleased their 'old man' no end. It seemed to be good for him.

And if it made him smile at them, instead of shout at them, it could only be good for them too.

Anything that made him happy with them rather than hard on them could only be rated as an improvement!

"Saved. Saved?" The voice of Thomas was the first to shatter the stunned but sort-of-sacred stillness which had descended upon the little bedroom as he reechoed the word his dad had used. As though there was something magical, mystical, about it.

"You say you are saved. Does this mean there will be no more drinking, Dad?" Having broken the peculiar silence Thomas made bold to follow his initial repetition of the pertinent word with an enquiry into the scope of its power.

"Yes, son. It does." The dad-in-the-bed replied, simply. "It means that from now on there will be no more drinking. No more gambling. No more bars. And no more 'bookies'!"

No more drinking! And no more gambling!

Now that was some statement, coming from Tommy Martin!

A man whose whole life had revolved around betting and boozing!

It was just too big a pill for David to swallow, though.

"You tell us there will be no more drinking and no more gambling, Dad," he retorted, after a short and trying-to-come-to-terms-with-it pause. "No bars and no 'bookies'. How have you changed?"

It was what all three sons wanted to know.

And even though he had said it, how could they be sure of it?

Tommy Martin, though only a mere 'babe in Christ', had no illusions about his own inability to keep himself in the Christian pathway. But he had every confidence in the power of God to keep him there.

"I haven't changed myself, David," their dad went on to explain, addressing his specific answer to the specific questioner, but the message was meant for all. "I COULDN'T change myself. But it is the Lord Jesus who has changed me. And I am depending on Him to help me and to keep me. He will, too! You will see!"

It would be great if He **could** help their dad!

And keep him off 'the bottle'. And out of 'the bookies'.

It would be wonderful if it worked!

Their dad had said they would 'see'.

And so they would!

Only time would tell!

6

NEW LIFE IN THE OLD MAN

'You will see!' Tommy Martin had told his bemused boys that evening in the bedroom.

'You will see!'

And they did see! And so, too, did many other people in the town of Lurgan.

The radical change in the life of Tommy Martin affected the lives of three widely different groups of people. In three widely different kinds of way.

The first group to be affected were Tommy's drinking partners across the town.

Very shortly after he was saved the new convert received payment of a compensation claim for a back injury sustained at work about a year before. In his if-you-have-it-spend-it drinking, gambling days.

When news of the amount of the settlement filtered through the pubs-and-clubs grapevine, there was much speculation, and not a little eager anticipation, amongst Tommy's once-upon-a-time boozing buddies.

Five thousand pounds! FIVE THOUSAND POUNDS!

The forecast was that 'Tommy Martin will not only spend all his time drinking in the Windsor Bar now. He will probably **buy** the place!'

They had heard that Tommy had 'turned good-livin'' but they thought that with such an unheard of sum of money in his hand he couldn't resist the temptation to turn back for a tipple or two. He would be back in the bars in no time!

But they were wrong!

What they failed to understand was that Tommy Martin was now a totally different person from the hard-drinking card-playing short-tempered man they once knew.

He was a new creation. Completely.

Somebody who had started to read the Holy Bible instead of the racing forecasts.

And somebody who seemed much happier now in a church or a 'wee meetin'' than in a drinking club or a card-school.

To them Tommy Martin would always just be 'the wee wino from James Street'.

They couldn't understand it. At all.

And they didn't like it! One bit.

Tommy's three sons were another group to be instantly and significantly influenced by their dad's conversion. The impact on the lads, and their lives, was immediate. And lasting.

From the moment 'the old man' told them he had 'got saved' they saw an almost unbelievable change in him.

'The old man' began to live a new life.

Father didn't shout his instructions at his sons any more.

He shared his thoughts with them.

Father stopped cursing at them. And started counselling them.

Father didn't spend all his pay on himself any more.

He began to spend money on his house. And his sons.

Instead of beer he bought bread.

Instead of cigarettes he bought clothes.

Instead of placing bets he replaced beds.

It was amazing.

The most unexpected treat of all for the family, though, came with the compensation payment windfall.

Tommy Martin didn't buy The Windsor Bar, as had been predicted, but he did take all three of his boys 'up the town' in Lurgan one Saturday morning and bought each one of them a new bicycle.

What a shock and surprise for the growing lads whose only shared bicycle was a home-built job they had tinkered together on an old frame they had found on a dump. Their 'bike' had two wheels of slightly different size. The back one was marginally larger than the front which meant that the 'cyclist' was forced to lean forward on the saddle with the springs and stuffing sticking out of it, as he rode. This machine was propelled by an ill-fitting chain which kept falling off at inappropriate times.

It had no lights. No mudguards. Or no brakes.

So it should never have been used at night. In the wet. Or down a hill. But it was. All three. All the time!

That jalopy had absolutely no chance of meeting any standards of safety or comfort whatsoever!

But it was theirs. All their own work. All for their own use. And it lay spread across the footpath outside number 10 James Street in all weathers. And all the time, when not in use.

The boys weren't worried about anybody stealing it.

For who would want it? What would they do with it?

Now their completely changed father had bought each of them his very own bicycle. And what was more, each one of the new bikes was a different colour, so that there could be no disputes. About ownership. Or maintenance. Colour-coding had come to the Martin household.

David had a blue bike.

Colin's was red.

And the one Thomas chose was bright yellow.

How the fourteen-year-old loved his new bike. It was his pride and joy.

The three sons hadn't understood what their dad had meant that night in the bedroom when he told them that he had 'got saved'.

They were beginning to appreciate the effects of it now, though.
And they did like it! A lot!

Their dad had told them they would 'see'.

He had been right. And seeing was believing!

The change in Tommy Martin's lifestyle had another and purely
personal effect on his son Thomas, too. A deeper, and more profound
outcome. For as well as making him feel thankful it forced him to
think. To contemplate the kind of power it had taken to transform a
totally thoughtless drunkard into a thoroughly thoughtful dad.

Thomas also began to consider all these new things his father
had started to talk about. For as well as acting differently he seemed
to have learnt a whole new language! In addition to reading his Bible
and praying every day, he had now started to use strange words like
Saviour, redemption, atonement, heaven, hell, eternity, and
judgement. If being saved was such a real thing, surely there must
be something real about all these other concepts, too.

The pensive teenager promised himself he would give these
matters some real thought. Some other time.

In the meantime, however, he discovered that there was another
crowd of people out there who had also been touched by Tommy's
transformation. And some of them knew his dad's new words too!
They spoke the language!

For as well as the drinking pals who didn't understand the
apparent about-turn in their former pub-crawling partner at all, and
the grateful sons who didn't fully understand but were pleased with,
although forced to ponder, their delivered dad, there was a third group
who were mildly, if not mightily, affected by the well-known 'wino's'
conversion.

They were the family's friends and neighbours. The residents
of James Street and beyond.

And within this group there were two categories.

Firstly, there were those who just marvelled at the change in
their neighbour's life. Many of them gradually became friendly with
somebody to whom they had never spoken a word in their lives.
Most of them had been scared of him, barricading themselves in
behind closed doors until he went bawling by.

Now they spoke to him in the street. And smiled at him.

Then invariably, too, he would smile back. And start talking to them about the weather. Or their work. Or their worries.

How things had changed!

Others of their friends and neighbours, the second sub-division, were those who, led by the intrepid Elsie, had a novel message for the new believer. For they themselves were Christians. And young Thomas was astounded to discover that there were so many of them about!

Elsie was the first to tell the man to whom she had shown such prolonged and practical uncomplaining consideration that his salvation was 'an answer to prayer'.

"I have been praying for you ever since the very first day I met you, Tommy," she told him, obviously delighted. "I have been praying that God would save you. And now He has! Praise His Holy Name!"

Then there were others. Others who could easily understand the change that salvation had brought about in the life of Tommy Martin. For it had brought about a similar change in their lives at a time, also.

A variety of people approached the new Christian in the area, but they all seemed to have something the same to tell him.

"We have been praying for you for years, Tommy," they informed him, feelingly.

Up until that time Tommy Martin had known nothing about prayer. Or the power of prayer.

But now he knew. And he was going to need more prayer. Plus more power. In the days to come.

Somebody said to him one day, paraphrasing the words of Jesus to Peter who had been going through a bad patch at the time, "Tommy, I have prayed for you. That your faith won't fail."

Tommy thanked him, although he hadn't really a clue what the well-meaning man meant.

But he would soon find out!

7

FIRE AT THE FACTORY

The big test for Tommy the Christian, and Colin, Thomas and David, the teenagers, came in the summer of 1977.

Tommy had been saved for almost a year and had continued to be a marvel to many. There were still dozens of people in the town who said they 'just couldn't get over the way Tommy Martin has changed'.

His three sons hadn't changed much, though.

They were still meeting their mates, roaming the streets, and of course building the annual bonfire.

It was the afternoon of Friday, July 8th, 1977, and so there were only three more full bonfire-building days to go until lighting up time on the Eleventh Night. Thomas, his brothers, and their friends were up in the centre of Lurgan collecting all kinds of combustible junk, when somebody shouted, "Look at all that smoke! There must be a fire over at our place!"

A sudden sinking feeling struck the stomach of every busy bonfire builder.

"The bonfire!" somebody else yelled, giving instant expression to everyone's instant reaction. "It's the James Street bonfire! Some Catholic has lit it on us!"

Big tyres and broken branches were immediately abandoned, and the three Martin lads and their friends all ran as hard as they could back to their own street. No-one stopped for breath. No-one ever thought of stopping for breath. This was serious non-stop stuff!

Somebody had set their bonfire alight! And they had to see who it was, there and then!

As the gasping group turned the corner into James Street, though, they suddenly realized that there was more than their bonfire alight!

The Thompson Rodgers paper factory was on fire!

Having stopped for a break to regain their breath, and to try and grasp the gravity of what was actually happening before their eyes, the gang of lads set off again, at full speed.

They were stopped short by the intensity of the fire.

For the fire had become an inferno.

Huge reels of paper made towering torches, their flames licking up to the sky. Stacks of scrap paper, waiting to be processed, had become monstrous mounds of fire.

The heat was horrendous.

There was a suffocating smell of smoke.

Suddenly, somewhere deep in what had once been the factory, a gas cylinder exploded, shooting showers of sparks and burning debris high into the air. Fanned by the strong wind all those sparks and shreds of burning cardboard were soon raining down on the surrounding streets and houses.

It didn't take the mesmerized Martins long to realize that this fire was going to have a dramatic effect on their future lives.

The James Street bonfire had been set alight by a steady stream of stray sparks.

That was bad.

The Thompson Rodgers factory was now a furious inferno. So their father would be out of a job for a while, at least.

That was worse.

As they stood there, transfixed in the street, as close to the conflagration as the searing heat and busy firemen would allow, Colin, Thomas and David became aware that something even more catastrophic than the burning of a bonfire or the loss of a job was also taking place before their very eyes.

Their own house was on fire.

That was worst of all.

Father had always told everybody how wonderful it was to be so close to his work.

Not so fine though when the paper factory went on fire!

After standing in shock for a few minutes, Thomas spotted his father at the edge of the crowd.

"Come on boys! Da's over there!" He had to shout to make himself heard over the roar of the fire and the hiss of the hoses.

The other two boys didn't have to be told twice. All three of them set off spontaneously, elbowing their way through the crowd of curious fire-watchers.

When they reached their dad they found him devastated.

His face, where not red with the heat was smutted with soot, which in turn was tracked with tears.

On discovering that his three sons had pushed up beside him, Tommy Martin instinctively slid his arm around David, the youngest, and said sadly to all of them, with the air of someone accepting the inevitable, "The Lord is burning my past, boys! He had to!"

This was a crisis in the new Christian's life.

It seemed a savage blow to a father, who, after years of failure, was attempting to establish a home for his family.

And the fire which left their home a smouldering shell also destroyed something so singularly precious to Thomas. It had once been his pride and joy. It had once been his yellow bike.

When the firemen were hosing down the smoking remains of what had once been number 10 James Street, Thomas picked his way carefully through into what had once been their backyard. There he found, lying where he had left it, against a wall, all that was left of his bright yellow bike.

The saddle was charred. The tyres were gone. The frame was blackened. The wheels were buckled.

What had for the past ten months been the apple of his eye was now nothing more than a heap of scrap. It was useless for anything. His beautiful bike was just so much scorched and mangled metal.

Later on that evening Thomas and his brothers were left wandering about in the street outside what was left of their home, in a state of sullen, silent shock.

They didn't quite know what to say, either to each other or to anybody else.

It was then that one of their friends decided to give the bewildered brothers a bit of good news. Something to cheer them up.

He made his way right up beside Thomas who was standing, hands in pockets, staring blankly in through the softly smoking aperture which just that morning had been their front window.

"Never worry Thomas," the well-meaning pal began seriously, "New Street have agreed to help us build our bonfire up again before The Twelfth."

Thomas stood motionless. Desolate. Detached.

He could not believe it!

Continuing to gaze fixedly in through what had once been the 'front room' window, he saw the shambles on what had once been the 'front room' floor.

The roof had caved in. So there were slates mixed up in the mess.

The upstairs had come down. And all that remained of what had been their dad's dressing table, the metal frame of the mirror, was mixed up in the mess.

The bits that weren't still stubbornly smoking were by then either charred to ashes or soggy with water. Or both.

But New Street were going to help them rebuild their bonfire!

The Martin family had lost everything.

Their home was gone.

Their clothes were all gone.

Their furniture was all gone

Their money, what little they had of it, was all gone.

Their treasured bikes were all gone.

Their dad's job was gone...

But they shouldn't really worry. For New Street were going to help them rebuild their bonfire!

Thomas felt sick.

A bonfire was about the last thing in the wide world he wanted to see at that particular moment! He reckoned he had seen a big enough bonfire that day to do him for the rest of his life!

He felt sick.

Then, after a few days he began to feel very sad.

And in a week or two's time he began to feel really mad. And bad. And bitter.

Why had the God who had saved his dad and made him so happy, allowed this to happen to them?

8

GOING WILD

The Martins were homeless. But not for long.

Their first move after the fire was to Hill Street, but they only stayed there a short time before being allocated a bigger, better house in Trasna Way, in Lurgan's predominantly loyalist Mourneview estate.

After the horror of the fire and the hassle of the flits, Thomas Martin turned his back on God, and all things religious.

He was determined to enjoy himself.

So there would be no more Christian Endeavour. No more choir. No more church.

He was going to live life to the full, doing what he wanted, how he wanted, when he wanted.

Thomas and David became part of a gang of a dozen or more loyalist youths who roamed their own estate, and the town of Lurgan at night. Every night of the week.

They began to attend discos all over the town and district. Any night of the week. Smoking, drinking, swearing, and fighting had all become an essential feature of Thomas Martin's new 'going wild and running free' lifestyle.

And his heartbroken father blamed himself.

How could he ever expect his sons to behave any differently from the example he had set for them for the greater part of their lives?

All he could do was pray for them. And this he did, diligently. Earnestly. Continually. It was not unusual for Thomas and David to come sneaking into the house at two o'clock in the morning, and as they crept past the living-room door on their way up the stairs, to see their father down on his knees at a chair, pleading out loud with the Lord for his boys. He was begging God to spare their lives, and save their souls.

When Thomas started to frequent the Windsor Bar, many of his father's former drinking partners recognized the seventeen-year old. And had a special seat for him.

"That was the stool your father always sat on, son," a regular customer told him one night, "so every time you come in here it will be yours!"

They kept their word to him, too.

It was a cruel irony, and extremely distressing for Tommy Martin who had been saved and hadn't darkened the door of the Windsor Bar for more than two years, that his sons were taking his place. And Thomas had even succeeded to his stool!

In reflective moments Thomas considered his father. And what his behaviour was doing to the apparently rapidly ageing man. He always managed to banish the sharp arrows of conviction from his mind, though, with the thought, 'The old man enjoyed himself to the full. Then he got saved. So what's to stop me doing the same thing? I will enjoy myself to the full, and then get saved when it suits me. But not now. Not yet."

It was a dangerous philosophy, but the young renegade had never ever even once considered the possibility of sudden death. He was more concerned with enjoying every second of life.

This desire to see more and more of the world and its ways soon found Thomas and David being invited, by some of the older members of their gang, to attend house parties in Portadown.

Unknown to the two unsuspecting late-teenagers these functions were held for three reasons. It was for two of these reasons that they had started to go to the parties in the first place.

There was an unlimited, and unlicensed, supply of alcohol at all these parties.

That appealed to them.

There was a steady supply of drugs at all these parties.

That appealed to them too.

It was only after they had begun to frequent a number of these always late-night and often all-night parties in the late seventies that the two brothers discovered that there was a third, and more sinister, motive for them.

These smoking, drinking, drugging gatherings were recruiting stations for various loyalist paramilitary organizations.

For almost three years Thomas and David spurned all advances, and resisted all pressures to join up. They made excuses.

"We are far too young," they said.

"We have very little money," they said.

"We have absolutely no experience," they said.

None of these pretty lame excuses impressed the local warlords.

Age, they were informed, didn't come into it, and as for money and experience, both would be provided when needed.

Secretly, though, the lads had another, and truly genuine, reason for not joining up. They knew their dad wouldn't like it. He would be devastated, again, if he heard. And they had by then come to hold him in high regard even though his consistent living and constant praying sickened their happiness at times.

In the spring of 1981 the calls to sign up increased. In frequency. And in fervency.

Ten I.R.A. men had gone on hunger strike in the Maze Prison.

Rioting and looting had ensued in Belfast and Londonderry. Businesses were being petrol-bombed. Vehicles were being hi-jacked and burnt. People 'on both sides' were being killed, or maimed.

The loyalist paramilitaries had now begun to recruit in earnest. Long gone was the 'Don't worry we will talk to you again next month' kind of easy take-it-or-leave-it approach.

Attitudes had hardened alarmingly.

The rhetoric had become more resolute.

They were now mobilizing their members for what they had predicted would be the 'Doomsday Battle'. This, they forecast, would be the battle to end all battles. It would be their last stand for their 'loyalist heritage'.

But they needed recruits. Badly. And quickly.

So in late March 1981 Thomas Martin and his brother David succumbed to the pressures. They relented. And answered 'the call'.

They signed up in a house in Portadown.

For they wanted to 'defend their country'

And so they joined the Ulster Volunteer Force.

The U.V.F.

9

YOU'VE GOT THE WRONG BOYS!

Having become members of an illegal organization, Thomas and David Martin were now determined to do what they could to further the 'loyalist' cause.

What they didn't know, though, something they were blissfully unaware of, was the Royal Ulster Constabulary had been monitoring their movements for months.

From early in 1981, when the two young Martin men began to spend more time with the godfathers of the U.V.F., and appear more frequently at the parties in Portadown, the police began to observe them closely.

They knew that Thomas and his younger brother had either joined the U.V.F., or were about to join. For a few months they couldn't quite determine which. So they hung back. Watched. And waited.

Over the summer, however, their suspicions were confirmed. Thomas and David had started to become involved in terrorist activity. They weren't yet fully-fledged front-line bombing-and - shooting terrorists but they had become part of the support network. It was their job to function as drivers and couriers, ferrying paramilitary personnel or their illegal arms, from place to place.

Thomas and David were 'learning the ropes'. Serving their apprenticeship.

When the police had collected what they considered to be a significant dossier of information on the two trainee terrorists, they decided to act. To move in. And move them out.

Just before six o'clock in the morning on Monday 19th October, 1981,Thomas stirred uneasily in bed. He had been jolted into consciousness by the ominous roar of police Land Rovers pulling up, just outside the house. The throb of their engines, and then, after they had come to a stop, the rumble of many voices, seemed to echo, then re-echo, through the morning stillness. It sounded as though some sort of a siege was about to begin.

Thomas was terrified. His blood had all of a sudden started to run cold. He lay motionless. Stiff. Like a person paralyzed.

He knew what the noise was. And he knew what it meant.

In what seemed ages, but what was in fact only a matter of forming-up-outside minutes, there came an unceremonious hammering on the front door. This was no genteel push-the-bell-and-stand-back apologetic advance. It was more of the, 'if-you- don't-open-this-door, right now, we-will-break-it-down-for-you, right now, like-it-or-not-we-are-coming-in, approach.

Thomas heard his father's bedroom door open and the 'old man' starting to struggle down the stairs. And struggle it was.

Tommy, too, had been startled awake by the clamouring outside, and he had been nearly startled to death by the hammering on the door. He had pulled a pair of trousers on over his pyjamas and his descent was a half-awake balancing act. With one hand he was endeavouring to buckle the belt, to try and hold up the trousers, and with the other he was holding on to the banister, to try and hold up himself.

"All right! All right! I'm coming!" he yelled from the bottom step.

When he had crossed the hall, Tommy Martin unlocked the door. But he didn't have to open it.

With an almost explosive force the door burst open, and the bewildered father was confronted with what appeared to be a barrage of policemen.

"Do Thomas and David Martin live here?" one of them growled.

"Yes, they do," Tommy replied. He was mystified.

"What do you want my boys for?" he wanted to know.

"It's not us that wants them, mister," one of the officers retorted. "It's the detectives over in Gough Barracks in Armagh would like a word with them. Are they upstairs?"

Then, without even waiting for an answer to his question, the leading policeman, helped by a second, hustled Tommy Martin to one side. And the pair of them mounted the stairs. Two at a time.

Thomas was lying petrified in the bed. He hadn't moved a muscle since he had heard the police vehicles arrive.

Suddenly his door was pushed open so forcefully that it banged into the wall, and almost bounced back.

"Are you Thomas Martin?" the man-at-the-front asked gruffly.

"I am," Thomas answered, quietly.

"Thomas Martin, I am arresting you under the Prevention of Terrorism Act," the policeman went on.

Then the second officer took over. "You may as well get out of there and pull some clothes on," he ordered. "For you are coming with us".

Knowing that it would not be in his best interests to refuse such a demand, Thomas dragged himself out of the bed.

Trying to play the man, and mask the terror that had gripped his heart, he asked, with an air of defiance, "I am coming with you. And what am I coming with you for, I would like to know?

The answer Thomas was given was much the same as the one his father had been given, five minutes earlier. "The detectives over in Gough Barracks want to see you about one or two little matters," he was informed.

When his two policemen had bundled him out on to the tiny landing, David and his two policemen had arrived in the hall. Looking down, from the second step Thomas was disgusted with himself when he saw the state of his father.

Tommy Martin had steadied himself with his back against the wall.

He was weeping inconsolably.

And he was wringing his hands in despair. And disbelief.

"You have got the wrong boys! You have got the wrong boys!" he kept repeating. Over, and over, and over again.

It was all he seemed to be able to say.

As he passed him, one of the policeman possibly felt a twinge of sorrow for the demented old mad. Perhaps he was a father himself, but he was also confident that no mistake had been made, for he said, in a stage whisper, "No, Mr. Martin. We have got the RIGHT boys!"

As the Land Rovers roared away, Tommy Martin looked a shocked, pathetic figure, standing at the door. What was going to happen to his 'boys'?

What did happen was that they were taken to Gough Barracks, Armagh, and interrogated for three days.

Then from there they were transferred to Crumlin Road Prison, in Belfast.

Tommy's boys had been remanded in custody, charged with possession of illegal weapons, and membership of a proscribed organization.

10

CRUMBLING ROAD

When Thomas Martin stepped out of the prison van in the yard of Crumlin Road jail he was scared. Intimidated. Frightened. The great bleak block of a prison building seemed to obscure the sky. And the thought of spending an indefinite period in it, on remand, struck terror into his heart.

As he and David were marched in, to be allocated a cell, Thomas was appalled at the run-down state of the place. The corridors were old, and tiled, and cold. The plaster on the wall, where there still was plaster on the wall, was cracked, and mouldy. A heavy musty smell pervaded the place. 'Crumlin Road', Thomas thought as he was directed through a maze of corridors. 'So this is Crumlin Road. Looks more like Crumbling Road to me.'

If his first impressions of the place were not terribly encouraging, his first encounter with its inmates was even worse.

When they were interviewed by the prison officers, Thomas and his brother, the new boys in the block, were faced with a stark choice. "Do you want to be isolated?" an officer asked Thomas. "Or do you want to go to one of the paramilitary wings?"

He didn't much fancy being isolated, for he knew what to expect of isolation. It could be lonely. Forbidding. Uncertain.

He didn't fancy a paramilitary wing either, though. But for a different reason. He didn't know what to expect of them. How would he be accepted in there? Fair enough, there would be company. But what kind of company? The end of that option, too, was rather uncertain. It could be dangerous to go in there. It might mean misery.

Having thought about it for a minute or two Thomas decided to opt to be sent to a paramilitary wing. He would take his chance with them. And it was then that the two brothers were separated. David had also chosen to be housed with the other paramilitary prisoners, but he was allocated to 'A' wing, and Thomas was to be detained in 'C' wing.

When he was led away again, into a paramilitary wing of the prison this time, to be assigned to a cell, Thomas Martin became aware of a creeping sense of evil. He sensed that there were strange forces at play in here, that he had never encountered before. It seemed as though there were eyes watching him from every mouldy brick. And from every dusty cobweb. He had read somewhere once about Christians being thrown to the lions. This was the way they must have felt, he felt.

No wonder he was petrified. He had every right to be. For when he reached 'C' wing it was exercise time. All the loyalist prisoners on the wing were out in the prison yard. And the new and nervous prisoner was given a rather rough baptism into the rigours of prison life. For the prison officer just opened the door into the yard, gave him one mighty shunt forward, saying, "Away out there and see if them boys want you or not!"

As he catapulted into the exercise area three men broke off from their walking round and approached him. Then another, from a more distant part of the yard joined them. Now Thomas Martin, not yet twenty years of age, found himself standing, hoping they didn't see the shaking he could feel, being glowered at, and through, by these four crusty-looking characters. He was conscious, too, that the pace of the circuit of the yard by the other prisoners had dramatically decreased. It was not so much a military walk now, but more of a mechanical shuffle. All eyes, including those of the duty prison officers, were focussed on the solitary figure in the middle of the yard.

The whole atmosphere was menacing. Tense and terrifying.

Then the interrogation began. This time, though, it was not by the police but by these four men, who were, Thomas was soon to discover, the commanders on the wing.

As the questions flew in rapid succession, Thomas was always aware that an unacceptable response from him could bring an instant, and painful reaction from his interrogators. A punch or a kick would be mild. It could be worse. These men who were bombarding him with questions hadn't been arrested for shop-lifting. Many of them had been charged with violent crime. They were vicious criminals.

"Where do you come from?" they asked.

"What U.V.F. Company were you in?" they enquired.

"Who was your commander?" they probed.

"Who do you know?" they wanted to know.

On and on went the questioning. And Thomas was never sure what they were thinking. Or how he was doing.

Would he be accepted on the wing? Or given a hiding? It had happened he had heard.

The crude cross-examination lasted for almost ten minutes. Then there followed a silence which was so tangible it could almost be touched. The mechanical shuffle all around had come to a complete stop.

What was going to happen now?

Thomas didn't know. He could only wait.

After a short exchange, which had been accompanied by a solemn nodding of heads, between the four interrogators, one of them said, "O.K. young fella. Start walking round there."

A sense of relief flooded over Thomas.

He was in prison, and he was mad about that.

But he had been accepted on to 'C' wing by some of the most ruthless commanders in the prison. And he was glad about that.

When Thomas joined the loose line of prisoners parading around the yard the pace of the procession picked up again.. It was obvious that the free entertainment was over for that particular evening.

It was now the turn of the other prisoners to ask this new boy a few questions.

For they not only wanted to know all about this reinforcement in their ranks, but they were just itching to hear the latest news. What was **really** happening on 'the outside'?

After exercise Thomas went back in. To settle in.

He had to prepare to spend his first night in his new abode.

On arrival at his allotted cell Thomas discovered that he was expected to share it with two others. There would then be three of them in what had once been a single cell.

The cell was crammed with all the furniture it could possibly contain. Single cells normally had a single bed, a tin locker, a table and a chair. Their cell, however, had a set of bunk beds, **and** a single bed, a tin locker, a table and a chair.

Conditions were cramped in the extreme. The occupants had to take turns at sitting on the chair, and then resting on their bed, or bunk. For there was no room to do anything else.

Their only toilet was a grey-white pot, with a grey-white lid, hidden away in a corner. This had to be used by all three of them, and was emptied once a day. At 'slopping out' time.

This 'slopping-out' time was an hour every morning., and it was a busy hour. In that time all cell pots had to be emptied and returned, all prisoners had their turn in the antiquated washroom, and it was also breakfast time.

Republican prisoners had their hour out first one morning, loyalists the next. The prison authorities were careful to make sure that the two never mixed. For that could make for mayhem.

Apart from that one hour in the morning, those three men on remand were together in that cell for the remainder of the day, every other day. Twenty-three hour lock-up, it was called.

On alternate days they had exercise. Loyalists one day. Republicans the next. Thomas had been initiated into that routine on the day of his arrival. From 5.30 until 8.30 p.m. every other evening the loyalist prisoners were permitted to watch TV and walk round the exercise yard.

It was very late before Thomas and his new enforced companions settled down for the night on that first night. The new boy had a lot he wanted to ask his cell-mates about. And they, in turn, had a lot they were anxious to learn about him.

When they eventually did decide to try to settle to sleep, one of the other men in the cell had a piece of timely advice for its newest occupant.

"If you should happen to have to get up to use the pot in the middle of the night, Thomas," he cautioned, "beware of the cockroaches. They come in under the door there when the lights go out!"

It was sensible, practical, valuable counsel.

And for the first few virtually-sleepless nights, Thomas remembered it. And watched where he put his feet, sliding, rather than lifting them along.

Then when he became more familiar with his surroundings he forgot. And paid for it one night. He felt a squelch beneath his feet. The prickly-tickly sensation of a crunching cockroach on a bare foot on a cold cell floor was an unforgettable experience. But it was one which Thomas could hardly avoid repeating. For they were everywhere, those big black shiny beetles.

Two mornings later, when he and the other loyalist prisoners were first for slopping-out and washing-up, Thomas discovered that the washroom wash overrun with them too.

He had to scoop about twenty cockroaches as big as half-crowns out of the chipped Belfast sink, with the side of his hand and his forearm, to allow him to wash. They had crawled in over the edge during the hours of darkness, and were trapped in this steep-sided soap-encrusted thing. On hitting the floor they scattered in all directions. They would probably return that night again.

It would be the republicans turn to scoop them out tomorrow.

After his first few days of incarceration in this new location, Thomas decided that he must have been particularly unfortunate. Surely he had 'drawn the short straw'.

For his new address was Cockroach Corner, in Crumbling Road.

11

SOLITARY CONFINEMENT

Conditions in the decaying prison were so bad that the prisoners decided that since their constant complaints appeared to fall on continually deaf ears, they would have to do something about it themselves.

If the authorities weren't willing to provide them with more up-to-date facilities, then they would take the situation into their own hands. And make sure they had to.

In whispered conversations in the recreation room and exercise yard a plot was hatched which they felt would force officialdom to do something about their cramped conditions. The antediluvian washing facilities. And the twentieth century cockroaches.

The plan was that on a certain Sunday when 'A' and 'C' wings were being brought together to the morning service the prisoners would all at once turn on the prison officers before they actually entered the prison church, and by sheer weight of numbers overpower them. They would then barricade themselves into 'A' wing, run riot in there, and wreck it completely.

They intended to destroy everything. Smash the stinking sinks to smithereens. Bash up the beds. Rip up the mouldy mattresses. Cause mayhem.

Then, when all of that was over surely they would have to move them to somewhere else, or at least provide them with more modern showers, beds and bedding, where they were.

That was the simple plan. It had been concocted in secret. To be executed in public. On Sunday 6th December, 1981. And it was bound to produce an instant and acceptable improvement in their condition.

Or so they all thought!

But something went wrong. Somebody, somewhere had become suspicious. Perhaps the governor had somehow become sceptical of all those hardened gun-runners and bomb-planters who had suddenly and inexplicably developed a totally uncharacteristic interest in attending church! Or could a prison officer have overheard a whimper of a whispered conversation at one time or another? In the yard? On a corridor? In a washroom?

Whatever the reason, when the Sunday of the proposed wreck-in arrived, the officers departed from normal procedure when escorting the prisoners along to the morning service. Instead of opening a wing at a time and allowing a potentially uncontrollable influx of prisoners to the church, the officers only allowed four prisoners out of either wing at a time. When these men had been conducted into the church, then four more were allowed out, and so on, with the intervening doors being securely locked. Behind everybody. Every time.

This precautionary ploy meant that there was never an unacceptably dangerous ratio of officers to inmates, at any time. Thus the possibility of the officers ever being overpowered was averted.

The prisoners had been foxed. They were frustrated. And furious.

The pack-out Sunday service didn't do anything to ease the sickening sense of having been outsmarted. They were only there to create confusion. Deliver destruction. Trigger trouble.

And it hadn't worked!

Many of the would-be rioters were left seething. They couldn't let it rest at that. They wouldn't. And didn't.

Later in the week 'A' wing decided to go it on their own. One evening when they were being shepherded out for recreation they took a number of the prison officers hostage, and wrecked their wing. Destroyed it completely. As had been the original do-it-on-a-Sunday plan.

Some of them even climbed out on to the roof and sat there, hurling slates down into the prison yard, and ignoring all instructions or pleas to come in. Climb down. And give up.

Tommy Martin was shocked when he switched on the six o'clock News on the TV back in Lurgan that evening. For he instantly recognized one of the rioters on the roof. It was his David!

News of the anarchy on 'A' wing soon filtered through to the comrades on 'C' wing. And the command echoed down the corridors, "Loyalist prisoners! Barricade your cells!"

So they did.

Since all available prison staff had been mobilized to help repress the rebellion on 'A' wing, all other prisoners were on twenty-four hour lock-up. Objecting to this, and as a token of solidarity with the current commotion, all the loyalist prisoners did as they had been ordered

They bunged up the cell locks using any means they could manage. Or with any thing they could find. Then they piled all their furniture against the cell doors. So that nobody could get in, or out, for days.

These actions merely served to exacerbate, rather than resolve, the very explosive situation in the prison.

When eventually the riots were quelled and the block-in block-out protests were over, relationships within the prison were at an all time low. And tensions at an all time high.

Conditions for the prisoners didn't improve, in any way. Or on any wing.

Rather, they seemed to grow worse.

Sullen tempers simmered below the surface.

One day Thomas took exception to a remark from a prison officer. He didn't like what the man said. Or how he said it. His arrogant attitude annoyed the petulant prisoner. And he told him so. In no uncertain terms.

Soon verbal altercation gave way to physical confrontation.

Argument was replaced by action.

A fight broke out. And a free-for-all ensued.

Thomas was pulled back, pinned down, and then jostled, none-too-gently, away.

And into solitary confinement.

If his introduction to Crumbling Road had been both an emotional and physical shock to the system, his introduction to solitary confinement was to prove even more horrendous.

'Solitary' was served in a cold cell furnished only with a table and a chair. The base for his bed was a raised concrete platform, covered with boards. A mattress, which Thomas could use to cover the boards, to make his bed, was thrown into the cell every night at eight o'clock. And removed next morning at eight o'clock. This was to prevent the prisoner even contemplating lying around all day. There was no toilet, but there was, as ever, the perpetual pot in the corner. This was emptied at the whim of the officers, morning or night.

Although he was a heavy smoker at that time, Thomas was not allowed cigarettes in solitary. He didn't even have laces in his shoes. Just in case he should happen to dream up any novel ideas for their use!

The days were so long. And so silent.

The only sounds he heard were when the officers came to throw in his mattress. Or to remove it.

To set in his two-inch allocation of washing water. Or to take it out.

To take away his pot. Or to bring it back.

To hand in his food. Which was foul.

Or to collect the empties. Which was always.

Although the food was often far from appetizing, it kept him nourished. And he spent as much time as possible in the actual eating of it. For it gave him something to do to help while away the seemingly endless hours.

After his first day in solitary Thomas was arraigned. And given three more days.

He was forced to plan a pattern for passing three more miserable, lonely days. He had to. Otherwise he would have gone crazy.

Days were spent in a mixture of mental and physical activity. Thomas read. And he exercised.

His intellectual lifeline was the Bible.

On the solitary table in his solitary cell in his solitary confinement was a solitary Bible. 'Placed by The Gideons' it said inside it.

Thomas spent long periods reading that Bible. He didn't understand half of it and he could never see the sense of the pages and pages of lists of names and family trees he came across every now and again.

But there were other parts of it he liked. He discovered verses in the New Testament bit which he had heard his radically-reformed father quote to press a point. There were also passages which he recollected having heard in the Boy's Brigade, the Christian Endeavour, and as a reluctant choir boy in the Morning Service. All thanks to Elsie!

If reading the Bible helped keep his mind alert, walking round and round and round and round his cell kept his body fit. But it was so repetitive. So monotonous. So soul-destroying, somehow.

After four dreary days it was over.

Thomas was out again. Back into his cramped cell, where he at least had the company of the other two inmates who brought him bang up to date with all the latest prison gossip.

Since he was now back into normal routine, and not yet been sentenced, but was still on remand awaiting trial, Thomas had something exciting to which he could always look forward. These were regular events to eagerly anticipate.

They were his vital link with the big outside world. The safeguard of his sanity.

And these highlights happened just three times a week.

12

IT WILL ALL WORK OUT FOR THE BEST, YOU'LL SEE!

Those ardently-awaited, avidly-anticipated three times weekly events were the visits to Crumlin Road Prison of Tommy Martin, the ever faithful father of Thomas and David.

He came to visit them every Monday, Wednesday and Friday. Without fail. Like clockwork. Whatever the weather, and despite the difficulties, Tommy Martin never disappointed his prodigal sons.

The pair of prisoners sent out the visiting passes and their father took it from there. And it was no easy journey.

Tommy Martin had a Yamaha 80 step-through motor-cycle. And asthma.

So although he was determined to visit his sons, whatever the cost to himself or his health, Tommy's only mode of transport saw him out in all kinds of weather. And inhaling all kinds of toxic fumes.

In an attempt to avoid these harmful fumes which choked up his chest, and also to avoid being blown off his bike by some of the roaring juggernauts, Tommy kept to the back roads as far as possible.

On three days out of every week, the old man with the new life, and as it was to prove, unswerving loyalty, made it from Lurgan to Belfast and back, on a non-too-powerful bike, by a maze of minor roads.

All to visit his two prison-bound boys.

It would be impossible to assess the value of those visits. To the concerned father they provided a focus for the week. That was despite the fact that they represented both a challenge to his ailing health and a drain on his already meagre resources.

They were a lifeline in a stormy sea for his struggling sons, though. Their dad's visits were a godsend to them in any number of ways.

Their initial benefit was a very practical one. Every time he came to see 'the lads' Tommy Martin brought them something. In addition to the clothes which he had taken away, washed and returned, he always had a parcel for them. A treat for his boys. It was like The Lucky Dip. These goody-bags could contain a bar of soap, a sachet of shampoo, apples, oranges, or sometimes the most welcome surprise. Something new to wear. A pair of socks, perhaps.

The climax to the week always came at the end of the week. That was when each young man found that he had a copy of the Lurgan Mail in his parcel. Thomas used to read it from cover to cover. Ads. and all. Every week. It kept him informed about what was happening at home. Back in Lurgan.

The prison regime was an artificial environment. The local paper helped him keep tabs on reality.

The two young offenders, little more than teenagers themselves, looked forward to their dad's parcels in the same way as a five year old looks forward to Christmas.

"What will he bring me today?" each one wondered. Though in separate locations under the same roof, they were totally together in thought. And eager expectation.

It may have been childish. But it was fun. And a focus.

What they weren't to know, though, was that this unremitting kindness, and the constant comings-and-goings, were proving a financial burden on their 'old man'.

There were times when he was forced to sell some valued household items. Just to help make ends meet.

But the only One he ever told about his struggles was God.

And He never failed to provide the attentive father with both the stamina to keep going and the substance to keep giving.

Perhaps the greatest boon of all to be born out of this family trial was the bond it built up with a variety of different people. Their dad was like the connecting link in a bicycle chain. When he arrived for one of his visits the chain became complete. And felt as though it could power the wheels. Get everything up and moving again.

Tommy Martin, when he came, served as a vital contact between his two sons, and for each of them with the world which was spinning by. Just outside the walls.

Thomas used to be thrilled to hear him say things like, "I was talking to Mrs. Forus the other day, and she was asking for you."

This remark would immediately trigger a train of thought in his captive son's active mind. He would reflect on the fortunes of the Forus family.

"And what's her daughter doing now? You know, the smart one," he would go on. "Did she get a job or is she still at the College?"

Although physically detained inside, Thomas tried to dwell mentally on the outside. He took a keen interest in all his dad had to tell him. Then he reflected on it for hours at a time. There wasn't an awful lot else to do. Especially on twenty-three hour lock-up days.

An essential link that Tommy's visits helped to keep alive was the relationship between Thomas and David. One in 'C' wing. The other in 'A'. The two sons had so planned their dad's visits that he saw David first on one day. Thomas first on the next. This meant they could always ask about each other.

The second question Thomas usually asked his father, next only to, "How are you, dad?" was, "And how about David? How is he today?"

This bonding between father and sons was important. There was another bonding building up, too, that Thomas often heard his dad talk about, but found himself at a loss to fully understand.

It was all about prayer.

Without preaching at him, Tommy Martin's quiet Christian attitude affected his imprisoned son.

"We were praying for you and David in our wee prayer meeting last night," he would say every now and again.

Then on another time he would remark, almost casually, "Do you know this, Thomas, I was up the street in Lurgan on Saturday and two different people stopped me to ask me how you were? Before they left the both of them told me that they pray for you and David every night."

Invariably he would then wait to assess the impact of such initial observations before going on to ask, "Isn't that great? Isn't it very thoughtful of them?"

It was like the 'being saved' thing, Thomas concluded. If his father thought it was great, and it kept him happy, then it was great.

"Yes, it is indeed," he would agree, with something which seemed a lot less that outright enthusiasm. For he didn't dare let his dad know that he was touched inside more than he ever dared tell.

The praying he could see some sense in, but his dad often said other things that he couldn't figure out at all. He had a habit of remarking, whether it was to cheer his son, or himself up, Thomas was never quite sure, "This will all work out for the best, you'll see!"

This statement was occasionally accompanied by a smile. Occasionally by a sigh. Depending on the mood of the man at the moment.

On a day when his 'it will all work out for the best' declaration didn't encounter immediate opposition, Tommy went on to make the craziest comment of all.

"I believe the Lord has a purpose in you coming in here," he would claim, with remarkable confidence.

That was usually too much for Thomas.

He couldn't agree with that! No way!

And he said so, too!

A 'purpose' in him 'coming in here'?

With the cold and the cockroaches and the criminals and the solitary confinement!

A purpose in that!?

'Being saved' had been marvellous for the old man in a multitude of ways.

But sometimes he just seemed to carry it to ridiculous extremes!

13

CHAOS IN THE COURTROOM

After a year on remand the Martin men's solicitor visited them in September 1982 to tell them that their long wait was over at last. They were soon to know their final fate. Their trial date had been set for November of that year.

And what a trial it turned out to be!

It was the first of what were known as the 'supergrass trials'. A prisoner had turned 'Queen's evidence' and had agreed to testify against a number of his former accomplices. As far as the authorities were concerned, at the height of 'The Troubles', this would save court time for it had the potential of seeing a number of prisoners sentenced all at once.

However, as with many things in life and law, it didn't work out exactly as planned.

The court that day was jam-packed. It was crammed full.

Twenty seven prisoners had been brought to court for a preliminary trial. They were going to have their charges reviewed, or so they had been told. Thirteen men were confined in one dock. Fourteen were crowded into the other. The place seemed to be crawling with police and prison officers. The public galleries were full to overflowing.

The atmosphere was tense. Expectant. Explosive. Electric.

None of the prisoners were exactly enamoured by their one-time-ally who had decided to rat on them all. If they could have reached him they would have taken him apart, limb from limb, no problem. In the courtroom, there and then.

Tempers were high. Security was tight. And media attention was focussed on this landmark trial.

As the proceedings began the atmosphere in the courtroom became thoroughly unpleasant. Some far-from-complimentary remarks were exchanged between the prisoners and the supergrass who was giving evidence.

Then the inevitable happened. Seething anger burst forth into violent action.

A prisoner was returning from a toilet break which he had requested when the officer in charge of him laid a hand on him to urge him forward, back to his position in the dock.

Suddenly the uneasy silence was split wide open. 'Rent in twain from the top to the bottom'. "Don't you dare touch me!" the prisoner bellowed, and swung a punch at his guard.

Mayhem ensued.

As if on cue all the prisoners in both docks rounded on their guards. If only they could reach that sneaky supergrass!

First one out of the courtroom was the judge. From his position on the bench he took one long hard look at what had happened and probably had a fleeting vision of what could still happen, then beat it! Beetled away like a woodlouse exposed to the light. He scurried out through a back door as hard as he could go flanked by two flustered police officers!

Meanwhile back on the floor of the courtroom a full scale riot was in progress. Fists were flying. Feet were flying. Batons were being used in a frantic attempt to bludgeon the incensed prisoners into subjection.

Thomas Martin stood mesmerized. He had been in the middle of his dock and every one of his fellow-prisoners on its fringes was fighting furiously as though his life depended on it. But he wasn't involved. Not yet, anyway.

The prisoners sensed that the police were beginning to panic. One of the officers had broken away from the fray for he discovered that he had a distressing and potentially disastrous personal problem.

"My gun! My gun! I have lost my gun!" he kept wailing urgently to his embattled colleagues, most of whom were too interested it preserving their own reputation and facial features to be bothered with his self-inflicted dilemma.

The supergrass was hustled hastily and unceremoniously out of court. Essentially for his own safety.

As he surveyed the fracas, Thomas was enjoying the excitement and wondering who he could easily clobber to best advance the cause when his attention was attracted to something on the floor at his feet. He gaped in amazement.

It was the policeman's gun!

In all the confusion it had somehow become dislodged from its holster and was now lying on the floor of the dock. The frightening fact was that it had come to rest at the feet of a dozen or so men most of whom were standing there waiting angrily and aggressively to be tried for weapons offences!

An instant and evil thought flashed into the prisoner's mind.

If he could reach down and grab that gun what control he could command! And what damage he could do! But perhaps it would be just too risky. What if...?

His deliberations were brought to a sudden and dramatic stop.

A policeman, having spotted the gun, and sensing that Thomas had spotted it also, grabbed him firmly round the neck.

"All right, mate! All right, I'm not doing anything !" Thomas shouted, with a patently insincere air of innocence.

Then a mightily relieved policeman shoved an arm into the midst of a mass of milling feet and retrieved his missing gun.

Within twenty minutes the police and prison officers had regained precarious control of the situation and a kind of uneasy order was restored. The trial could no longer proceed , however, since both the judge and the chief witness for the prosecution were out of the courtroom and neither of them was demonstrating any burning desire to make an immediate return!

Realizing that their only hope of avoiding a repeat of the riot was to remove as many of the prisoners as possible from the scene at once, the security guards began to herd them towards the steps at the back which led down to a holding cell. One by one the restrained prisoners were either pushed, pulled or otherwise propelled down those steps and into that cell.

After each new admission the door was slammed shut and firmly locked.

There were already nine in the dark, damp and smelly cell, sitting glumly on the benches down both sides, when Thomas was launched in with such force that he thought he would be the first man to go straight out through the graffiti-adorned back wall.

Every two or three minutes the door would be unlocked and another prisoner projectile would catapult across the cell. As the bundle of bumped, bruised, bleeding and bawling bodies gradually increased the new arrivals didn't have so far to travel. They stopped at a buffer of bodies sooner.

When the cell was almost full Thomas realized that his brother David, who had been very much in the thick of things upstairs, hadn't yet shown up. Where was he? Or perhaps more importantly, **how** was he?

Those questions were answered four openings later.

David was shoved into the by-then-grossly-overcrowded cell, blood streaming down his face from a wound on the forehead. An already-blackening eye peered out from below a blood-caked eyebrow.

Later that evening, when the security presence both in and around the courthouse had been substantially reinforced, and the seething tempers of the men below had cooled only slightly, the most of the prisoners were escorted back to their more permanent quarters in Crumlin Road Prison. David and two others didn't go with them though. They were taken away to the hospital where David had two stitches inserted in the gash above his eye.

The authorities had been thoroughly disconcerted by the day's events.

Their supergrass trial had proved a superflop.

And the latest news filtering through to Thomas and his pals was that their key witness had retracted his evidence. He was refusing to testify against his former partners in crime ever again.

What was going to happen now?

That was what everybody wondered.

14

THE BLACKNESS OF DARKNESS

A few days later, on Tuesday 16th November, 1982, the trial was re-convened.

The prisoners who hadn't been sentenced in the previous fiasco were returned to court to have their trial completed. As they filed into court that day some of them looked as though they had been in a street brawl or a traffic accident. The parts of a few faces that weren't covered in adhesive plaster shone in brilliant blue-green hues.

Thomas Martin had a feeling that he and his thirteen fellow-prisoners who were due to be tried that day would suffer a backlash from the embarrassment of the fight on the floor, some days before. The authorities had now lost their key witness, the talked-up supergrass trial had tumbled down around their ears, and many felt that those who had already been sentenced had escaped with little more than token punishments.

Today would probably be seen as an attempt to claw back some credibility. And redress the balance.

His predictions were soon to be proved correct.

As the prisoners stood forward, one by one, to be sentenced, there were gasps and wails of shock and incredulity from the public gallery. Distraught relatives just couldn't believe the punishments that were being meted out to their loved ones.

When it came the turn of Thomas to be sentenced he stood forward stiffly, handcuffed hands held down before him. His ever faithful father sat stock still in the public gallery, gazing down blankly, as though turned into stone. He clutched a crumpled handkerchief tightly in his clasped hands.

There was a hushed, heavy silence as the judge solemnly read out the ruling of the court.

"Thomas Martin, you have been found guilty of firearms offences for which I sentence you to twelve years imprisonment," he began.

After a purposeful but momentary pause, to let the significance of that statement sink in with his astonished audience, he then continued, "You will also serve ten years for false imprisonment and you have, in addition, been found guilty of membership of a proscribed organization. For this you are sentenced to five years imprisonment.

This makes a total of twenty-seven years. These sentences to be served concurrently."

Thomas was stunned. His legs felt weak. The colour drained from his face. A feeling of nausea swept over him. Had he not felt so numb, so completely paralyzed, he was sure he would have been sick.

Twenty seven years in prison! The fact that the prison terms were to be served concurrently didn't mean anything to him at that time. He didn't fully understand what 'concurrently' meant. It was lost on him. All he could think of was TWENTY-SEVEN YEARS! He had just turned twenty-one. What would there be left in life for him in twenty-seven years time? When he was forty-eight?

And Thomas had got off lightly, relatively speaking. His brother David had just been sentenced to a total of thirty-four years in prison!

When the judge had finish pronouncing his sentence, Thomas stood thunderstruck, waiting meekly to be led away by his personal guard to serve out his term of imprisonment. Before going down the steps out of the dock he glanced at the public gallery, and there he spotted his father. Tommy. The 'old man'. His face was ashen. His eyes were red. He waved weakly to his sons. Thomas noticed, even in the fleeting glimpse he was permitted, the damp handkerchief in the waving hand.

Thomas was ushered out of the courthouse. Out and down. It seemed that they were never going to stop going down. When they did eventually reach the level again, the dazed and desperate prisoner was escorted through a long dimly lit tunnel, deep below the Crumlin Road.

It felt like the bowels of the earth. Reality had been left far behind with all the weeping and wailing relatives far above. There was an eerie, deathly, spooky silence down here.

As he walked along towards what was to prove to be the destination in that short, but apparently interminable downward journey, however, the uncanny silence began to be broken. By something even more uncanny.

What the new-man-to-the-block heard rent his already broken heart into even smaller, even more woeful, pieces.

It was pathetic. Plaintive. Poignant.

The first sounds Thomas heard in that unearthly underground holding centre were the sounds of grown men groaning. Some were sobbing softly. Others were wailing inconsolably.

Before he could take time to hear what it was one particular man was howling a small door was thrown open and Thomas was given a rough shove forward.

"In there!" the guard growled.

When Thomas stepped 'in there' the door was banged shut behind him.

The first thing that struck him about this cell, if it was a cell, he had been placed in, was its size. It was so small. Nothing more than a cubicle. Possibly four feet by four feet. About the size of a good broom cupboard. Or an outside toilet. But it wasn't as well equipped as a broom cupboard, or even an outside toilet. For there was nothing in it. Nothing at all. Just four cement walls. And a cement floor.

It was cold. A chilling dampness penetrated to the very core of his being.

Then there was the voice of the man next door. He was the one who had been wailing earlier. And he was still at it.

"What are we going to do?" he cried in deep despair. "What are we going to do? What are we going to do?" On and on it went.

Thomas knew the prisoner next door. He had been given ten years for a minor offence. This man was distressed, and felt he had every right to be. But he had been sentenced to ten years. Thomas had been handed down twenty-seven!

In a strange kind of way he was glad of this frantic man beside him. For the endless racket he was kicking up helped Thomas drown out the voice of the judge which kept ringing endlessly in his ears.

"Guilty. Guilty. Guilty," it kept saying.

"Twelve years. Ten years. Five years," it kept repeating.

"Away you go. Out you go. Down you go," it kept restating.

"You will be punished. And punished. And punished," it kept reminding.

Thomas sank down on to the cement floor, curled himself into a ball as best he could for heat. And it was only then that he discovered that he was shaking uncontrollably. His arms and legs were all aquiver.

The most terrifying thing of all to Thomas, though, worse than the wailing from next door, and even worse than the ringing accusations in his head, was the total blackness of that little cubicle. There was no light in it whatsoever, and the only chink of light he could see was a faint gleam below the door but he couldn't see anything by that. It was only a promise that such a thing as light did exist somewhere in The Far Away, but it had no place here.

This utter, total blackness struck abject terror into the soul of the newly-sentenced prisoner. He was scared to death. Frightened out of his wits.

Could this be what hell is like? he wondered more than once. Could it be any worse? The blackness of darkness, the wailing of the damned, the relentless accusations of wrongs, and the ultimate sense of judgment and punishment...

In that place, at that time, Thomas Martin reached the lowest point of his entire life.

'I will end it all,' he decided. 'I will commit suicide. Take my own life. I might as well do that as spend half of my days in jail. First time I get the chance I will poison myself, hang myself, shoot myself, take an overdose. Anything. Anyhow. But I will do it. End it. Finish it...'

Then he began to think of his father. His father who had visited him so faithfully. His father who had prayed for him day and night. And had got dozens of others to pray for him as well. His father who had told him that it was all going to work out for the best. He would see. Was this what he meant? This vision of hell?

But what would happen to him if Thomas did anything drastic?

Tommy Martin had suffered enough in his lifetime. What with the struggle of raising three sons on his own, many years and hundreds of pounds wasted on alcohol, the fire, and now this. If Thomas did what he was planning it would kill the old man dead. He would die of a broken heart, there was no question about that.

It was while Thomas was languishing in the blackness of darkness in that lightless, heatless, cheerless cubicle, that his devastated father arrived back at his home in Lurgan.

Colin, who had been waiting all day for news could hardly even wait until he was inside the front door before he enquired, "Well, Dad, how did it go today?"

Tommy sat down in the armchair in the living room before answering.

And when he did eventually reply it was with a note of utter dejection.

"It's going to be a long time before you see your brothers again, son," he said, in little more than a gruff whisper. "They both got big, big sentences. It's going to be a long, long time."

For the most of ten minutes he just sat there, motionless, as he had been earlier in the public gallery, like set in stone, just repeating over and over again, "A long, long time. Yes, a long, long time!"

He had hit rock-bottom, also.

His resolute faith in God was being thoroughly tested, again. And this time it was to the absolute limit.

It looked as though it was going to be, too.

For 'a long, long time' to come.

15

'THE BRIGHTEST LIGHT IN NORTHERN IRELAND'?

Officialdom, too, had a problem.

Now that the trials were over and the prisoners had been sentenced to what totalled to hundreds of years in jail, where were they going to put them all? And they had particular problems with Thomas, his brother David, and another man, all of whom were the youngest prisoners to be given such lengthy prison terms at that time.

Thomas had learnt by then that the 'concurrently' thing meant that he would only have to serve twelve of his twenty-seven years, and with remission that could be reduced even further. But where were they going to put him, even for the next six years or more?

These men couldn't be housed in the Hydebank Young Offenders Centre, for the maximum term which could be served there was a five year sentence. That wouldn't suit Thomas for he had been given twenty-seven years. And David thirty-four!

For two weeks these young prisoners waited while the authorities deliberated on what to do with them. Eventually they came to a decision.

Thomas and David Martin, and a third young man, were re-classified as 'long term prisoners'. This allowed the under-pressure prison administrators more scope in allocating these offenders to their permanent homes for the foreseeable future.

Where they chose at last to locate those three young men proved for them to be a real baptism of fire.

For they were sent to The Maze.

The fact that it could be seen from miles away at night and that it glowed like a beacon on the ground from aircraft approaching Belfast's International Airport, led to The Maze Prison being referred to, somewhat cynically, as 'the brightest light in Northern Ireland'.

This, though, was a complete misnomer.

It was anything but a bright light on the country's social or spiritual skyline.

By contrast, it was a hotbed of all that was evil. The Maze was a breeding ground of absolute animosity. Blatant bitterness blossomed there. Rank and unmitigated hatred were rife in there.

When Thomas Martin first arrived in the Maze Prison in early December, 1982, tensions between prisoners were running at an all-time high. And relationships had reached an all-time low.

Republican prisoners in the jail had come off their hunger strike and had finished their 'dirty protest'. They had lost ten men as a result of the hunger strike, hadn't achieved a lot by the dirty protest, and they were far from happy.

Their bottled anger and harboured resentment were then vented on the only soft target available to them. The loyalist prisoners.

Prisoners were not segregated in the Maze at that time and the republican inmates held a numerical advantage over their loyalist counterparts whom they outnumbered by the ratio of three to one. This numerical supremacy was utilized to maximum effect by marauding gangs of these merciless men who made lone loyalist prisoners, and especially **new** lone loyalist prisoners, the target of their savage attacks.

Many men had been trapped and brutally beaten before the guards could come to their assistance. Others were severely scalded by having buckets of boiling water thrown over them.

It was cruel, callous, and continuous.

It was ruthless, relentless, and endless.

Thomas and David learnt, and learnt fast, that there was a way to escape what they considered the ignominy of having to associate with republicans, and thus avoid their taunts and torment. It was to point-blank refuse to be housed anywhere near them, and if that failed, to cause as much disruption as possible, by wrecking their cells.

Prisoners who behaved in such an uncooperative fashion, they had been reliably informed by 'old hands', were accused of having broken the prison rules, and were subsequently classified as 'non-conforming prisoners'.

Although 'non-conforming' prisoners forfeited a percentage of their remission as a punishment for their pains, they were accommodated separately from the other prisoners. On the 'protest wings'.

Being housed away from militant republicans was the big thing. Whatever punishment might result was considered a small price to pay for either personal pride or personal safety, and why you were there depended largely on whether you were fiercely loyalist, or just dead scared.

From the day they arrived on the committal wing in their new prison abode Thomas and David put their pre-arranged plan into action. They immediately stated categorically that there was 'no way' they were going to be 'housed with any republicans'. Then they began to wreck their cells.

'Wrecking the cell' wasn't as drastic an action as it sounded, because the 'wrecking was not indiscriminate full-scale destruction. There were certain items that discerning prisoners didn't wreck. It would be stupid to bash up your table, your chair or your already fairly battered old tin locker, for instance. If you did this the guards would just shrug their shoulders and say, "Hard lines, mate. You can obviously do without one of those." So rather than being replaced it would be just left to lie where it was, as it had been left. And the protesting prisoner would be the only loser.

If, however, you lifted your chair and hammered and hammered at the window with the leg of it, until the glass splintered and shattered, or thumped and thumped at the 'virtually unbreakable' glass of the spy-hole until it eventually broke, for you hadn't really much else to do anyway, then that was a different matter. For windows without glass and unusable spy-holes constituted a security risk, and had to be replaced as soon as possible.

This caused the prison authorities both time and money, as well as serving them up an irritating helping of hassle and headache. So it was well worthwhile. And that is what Thomas and David did.

They bashed out their spy-holes, and banged out their windows. And then they waited. But not for long.

Very soon these two young reactionaries were re-classified. For the second time.

Thomas and his brother were now designated as 'non-conforming prisoners' and allocated cells on the 'protest wings'.

Before being transferred to yet another detention location the two men were given a chance to rethink their position, having been warned that they would forfeit ten days remission for every month they chose to remain on the 'non-conforming' protest. And that they 'would be deprived of certain other privileges'.

What the prison administration didn't recognize, however, was that they had placed these two young men into a position where they were about to be afforded one single, inestimable privilege.

The loss of ten days remission every month couldn't even begin to compare with the long-term benefits that this particular privilege had the potential to provide...

16

'AND WHAT ABOUT YOURSELF, TOM?'

It was on the 'protest wing' that Thomas Martin first encountered a number of prisoners who were to make a tremendous impact upon him. Both in the present and for the future.

These men had been housed in the 'protest wing' not because they were on protest, for they weren't, but because the republican prisoners in the main blocks had refused to have them. There was something distinctly different about this small group of prisoners. They brought with them a strange sense of submission to the authorities, and a resignation to their situation, which their republican counterparts found incomprehensible. This suggestion of what they considered a sort of spiritual spinelessness upset them in a way that they couldn't explain. And couldn't cope with.

The 'non-conforming' prisoners had volunteered to allow these men to be accommodated with them on the 'protest wing' since most of them were still regarded as loyalist prisoners. They were loyalist prisoners with a difference, however, for at some stage during their prison term they had come to know Christ as their Saviour. They told all who asked, and many more who didn't, that they were 'saved'.

These men were Christians.

He hadn't been many days in his new, and probably-permanent prison quarters, when Thomas picked out these men. They weren't hard to spot, either.

He first noticed them at exercise time, out in the recreation area.

They would play a game of football with the others for a while, and then half-an-hour before going-back-in-for-lock-up time they would hive off, and find themselves a quiet spot in a corner. There they would talk together quietly. For some reason or another they seemed to sit with their heads bowed for five minutes or so, too.

This newest 'non-conforming' prisoner found himself irresistibly attracted to this little group, just as others had found themselves instantly repelled by them. It took him a few days to identify to himself why he had been so magnetized by these men.

Then it dawned upon him! It was his dad. 'The old man'. They reminded him so much of his father! And he wanted to tell them so.

When he was talking to two of them one day, out in the exercise yard, he mentioned his father. The two men, who were relatively-recent Christians themselves, proved both attentive and responsive listeners. They soon realized that this new addition to their wing had two distinct needs. His immediate need was for someone sympathetic to whom he could talk, and his eternal, and indeed infinitely more urgent need, was to know the peace and joy that both they, and clearly this fellow's father, had found.

The two Christians listened with obvious interest as Thomas told them about his Dad. Nobody was in any hurry to go anywhere, so Thomas had time to tell of his father's former life, his conversion, his heart-break at his sons' prison sentences, his regular visits, and his persistent prayers.

"That's a wonderful story," one of them responded warmly, when he was sure that Thomas had finished. Then he went on to probe a little further. Press home an important point.

"And what about you, Tom?" he enquired with a genuine gentleness that touched the heart of Tom, as they knew him. "Are you a Christian, too?"

"No, I'm not. Not yet," Thomas was forced to concede, but his confession struck a pang of conscience deep in his own soul.

That initial contact proved to be the beginning of an increasingly rewarding friendship for Thomas.

Every day at recreation period he sought out some, or all, of the Christian group and began to spend more and more time with them. Thomas was moved by the manner in which these men treated him. They always made him feel welcome in their midst, and he in turn, began to feel more and more comfortable in their company. He felt safe with them, somehow. These men didn't seem to need to swear like some of the others, to make their point, nor did they seem to need to smoke either, like himself, to pass their time, or waste their money, or wreck their health, or calm their nerves, or whatever it was he did it for.

To Thomas Martin, a 'non-conforming prisoner' on 'the protest wing' of the Maze Prison in the early months of 1983, the simple companionship of these Christian prisoners was like an oasis in a desert. Being with them was like sitting in a warm room on a winter evening, with the hailstones bouncing off the roof, rattling down the chimney and fizzing in the fire. The storm was outside and remote, he was cosy and comfortable. Although not a Christian himself, Thomas felt more at ease in the company of these Christians than anywhere else. They gradually became, to him, a welcome refuge from the ways of wicked men.

When some of the Christian prisoners noticed this young man's attraction to their company and tolerance of their behaviour and beliefs they extended an invitation to him.

"Tom, we are having a wee meeting to study the Bible during recreation period tomorrow evening. We were wondering if you would like to come?" one of them asked, in a frank and friendly manner.

"Oh yes, I would love to go!" came the instant reply, and then Thomas found himself smiling to himself. He had begun to sound like his father, ten years before.

'The boys would just LOVE to go!' was what he had assured the persistent Elsie.

That meeting, to which Thomas actually looked forward, was to become the first of many during the next five or six months. He fast became one of their most regular attenders.

This new addition to the wee-meeting-study-group had little more than a superficial knowledge of the Bible. He knew there were stories in it he had heard at the B.B. and the C.E., courtesy of Elsie. These had been interesting to him as a boy.

There were stories about Noah and an ark, David and a giant, and Jonah and a whale. He seemed to recall too, there was a good one about some fellow called Daniel and a whole den of lions. Then there was Jesus who had done all sorts of wonderful things like turning water into wine, and raising dead people. There were some of His sayings, called parables, he remembered, too. His favourite of them by far, was the one about a sower out in the fields sowing seed. It reminded him of his happy year in Ardmore, somehow.

The expressed purpose of Jesus in coming into the world to die on a cross to put away his and everybody else's sins, though, was lost on Thomas. His father had tried to talk to him about it any time he was afforded even half a chance, but in those days Thomas had no time whatsoever for such 'uncool' considerations.

Now, by complete contrast, he was attending the prison Bible studies as often as he could. And when he was there he was impressed by two things.

The first of these was how happy all the participants in the group seemed to be in their faith, and how keen they seemed to be on, and knowledgeable they seemed to be about, their Bibles. They talked about things like justification, and sanctification, and predestination. These were words Thomas had never heard in his life before! Some of it was all double-Dutch to him.

The understanding attitude of the others in the group to this Biblically-basically-green recruit was the other factor which made a profound impression upon Thomas. They were always inviting him to join in and 'say something or ask something'. He did try, but he was sure he must have made some rather irrelevant statements or asked some rather nonsensical questions.

Nobody ever once asked him, however, 'Are you daft?' Or, 'Do you know nothing?' Nor did anybody ever chide him with caustic comments like, "We have already explained all of that last week!" No. Never once was there a response like that.

Thomas always had his comments welcomed graciously. And his questions answered fully, clearly, and patiently.

This acceptance by the group made Thomas feel even more confident in their company, and it helped him, in some small way, to come to terms with the prospect of spending years 'inside'.

The only aspect of his association with these considerate Christian prisoners that made Thomas feel uneasy was the question that some of them chose to ask him, at different times, as the opportunity arose. Although he never felt threatened or intimidated in the presence of these men, Thomas was invariably struck to the heart by this question, which always appeared to come after he had referred to the words or works of the most consistent Christian he had ever known, his father.

It was simply, "And what about yourself, Tom?"

17

'LET HIM IN!'

It was approaching mid-summer and that should have meant long sunny days and balmy summer nights. The prisoners in The Maze, however, knew nothing of ten-thirty sunsets. Lock-up came for them at half-past eight, every evening. The normal time-passers in lock-up were reading, writing letters, or listening to the radio. You could also spend time talking to your cell-mate if you had anything left to say to him.

On the evening of Monday, 13th June, 1983, Thomas Martin lay flat on his back on his top bunk reading a small booklet that one of the Christian prisoners had passed on to him on the previous day, the Sunday. He held it up above his head, at arm's length, and read every word of it carefully. Prisoners don't need to skim their reading for lack of time. They can read whatever it is they choose to read as slowly as they like. Or as often as they like.

Thomas wasn't merely reading this pamphlet to pass the time, though. He was reading it because he was interested in it.

The booklet had been written by someone called Noel Grant and had a picture, copied from an original painting, on the cover. This picture showed a man standing out side a closed door, knocking repeatedly. It was called 'Let Him In!'

The other occupant of the twin cell, Jim, was lying down also. On the bunk below. Since there was only the one chair in the cell, Thomas and his mate hardly ever bothered to use it, except to sit at the table to write letters. They usually spent most of lock-up lying on their respective bunks.

Jim had the radio on the floor beside him, blasting away.

Normally Thomas would have been listening to the radio with him, but on that particular evening he wasn't. The noise of it didn't even annoy him, he was so accustomed to it. And although he loved the pop music that was blaring from it, at full volume, Thomas didn't even hear it.

He was totally engrossed in his reading.

As he studied that little pamphlet slowly and carefully, it reinforced to the thoughtful man on the top bunk, many things he had heard, during the last seven years, from his father. And also in the past six months from the Christian inmates of the prison.

It told him to recognize that he was a sinner. Thomas had no problem doing that. His present position in a high security cell in a top security prison would surely contradict any claim he would care to make to being an angel!

Then he learnt how the Lord Jesus Christ had come to earth, to die on a cross, to take upon Himself the punishment for those sins, so that Thomas, and whoever else believed in Him, could be cleared of the guilt of their sin. And set free in Christ. They would even be regarded as though they had never sinned at all!

Thomas had heard this before. His father had tried, often in vain, to tell him. He had begun to listen to the other men in the prison, though, as they talked about it. They never seemed to miss an opportunity to speak to him about their Christian faith, and challenge him as to his own position, and because he felt so at ease in their company Thomas had gradually become more receptive to the message.

About ten o'clock Jim from below turned down the radio and called up, "Tom, would you like a cigarette?" He obviously was going to have one himself for he had swung off his bottom bunk and had stood up to lift a tiny shiny tin off the table.

Opening the tin, he offered it to his cell-mate.

Rather uncertainly, Thomas reached out. "Aye, I will have one, Jim," he replied to the offer, selecting a cigarette, almost reluctantly, from the outstretched tin.

As his companion took one himself and then proceeded to bang the tin shut and bang the end of the chosen cigarette a time or two on the back of it, Thomas went on to half-hint at the cause of his apparent hesitation.

"Thank you Jim. That is my last one," he said softly.

Jim wasn't stupid. He had been watching his companion for weeks now and he had the situation all summed up in his mind. Having observed the kind of material Thomas had started to read, and coupling that with his recent reticence to even have a cigarette, he had come to his own conclusion.

Looking his cell-mate straight in the eye, which he could do easily, for he was standing on the floor and Thomas was lying on the top bunk, he exclaimed, "You know, Tom, before long you are going to be a Christian!"

Little did he know it, but 'going to be a Christian' was exactly what 'Tom' was thinking about!

When he had stubbed out his 'last' cigarette, Thomas lay back on his bunk once more.

And started to read once more.

And started to think once more.

He reflected repeatedly on that verse from the Bible, upon which the message of the booklet had been based. It was Revelation chapter three and verse twenty, which read:-

'Behold, I stand at the door, and knock: if any man hear my voice, and open the door, I will come in to him, and will sup with him, and he with me.'

It was then that something dawned upon Thomas that he had never contemplated before. It was the fact that Jesus Christ, the Son of God, was standing just outside the door of his heart. And of his life. And of his whole existence.

The astounding thing was, too, that He had been there, knocking persistently, for more than twenty-one years, and Thomas had never even recognized it!

As he thought back to incidents in his earlier life he began to understand that Elsie, the B.B. and the C.E., his father's conversion and witness, and now latterly the consistent testimony of some of his fellow-prisoners, had all been knocks. Some of them had been more deafening than others, he had to admit, but all of them had been demanding that he open the door, and let the Saviour, Who was still on the outside, in.

There was only one problem, though.

Thomas began to doubt if Jesus would want anything to do with a renegade rebel like him. Was it not sort of decent people He wanted, and needed? He could appreciate that Jesus would probably be quite happy living in the hearts of respectable, upright people who dressed nicely, spoke nicely, prayed nicely, and paid nicely. But what use could He have for long-term prisoners?

It was just then, when these troublesome doubts had begun to threaten to side-track his determination to open the door of his heart to Jesus, that his eye caught a phrase in his 'Let Him In!' booklet. He had been leafing idly through it, deciding whether to read it all yet again, when the words, which had been printed in block capitals arrested his attention. Those four stark words held him in a vice-like grip.

They were from the centre of the verse he had read so many times that he almost knew it off by heart.

'I WILL COME IN', they stated, clearly, confidently, and concisely.

That was it. The problem was solved. That was enough for the prisoner in the pursuit of peace.

If God said it, He would do it.

There was a pattern prayer printed in the booklet. It was suggested that readers could use this prayer to invite the Saviour into their lives.

Thomas thought about using it but decided against it. He would use his own words and invite Christ into his life in his own way.

Closing his eyes, as he lay on his bunk, Thomas prayed silently, but with a simple, unsophisticated sincerity, "Lord Jesus, I am a sinner. You know I am a sinner. I believe that You died on Calvary's cross to put away my sin. Please come into my heart and save me now. Amen."

As he finished that heartfelt prayer, an inexplicable sense of peace and of freedom from sin enveloped Thomas Martin's soul.

True, he was still physically a prisoner. And would be for years.

But in his soul he was free. He had discovered spiritual liberty in Christ.

And that would last forever!

It was just after eleven o'clock. Thomas was saved. Satisfied. And thrilled beyond measure!

He knew that something miraculous had just happened to him. It was just so wonderful.

Jim hadn't been far wrong.

'Tom, before long you are going to be a Christian," he had predicted.

Thomas thought, 'I should tell him.'

Then he wondered, 'Should I tell him?'

Leaning over and peering down, he saw that his cell-mate had already settled down for the night.

Thomas, though, was just full of his new faith and inner freedom. He was like a packed-full bud about to burst open and spring the beauty of its floral fragrance on an unsuspecting world.

He would have to tell Jim, or somebody, or probably even everybody, about it.

But that would have to wait until morning, now...

18

'MORNIN' TOM!'

Having vowed to tell Jim that he had become a Christian, first thing in the morning, Thomas curled up and fell fast asleep. And had the most refreshing night's sleep he could remember having for some time!

He felt so calm, so content, and so at ease with God, the world, and himself. The burden, and the shadow, of his sin had disappeared.

When Thomas eventually awoke next morning, Jim was up and about.

"Good mornin', Tom!" he greeted his semi-somnolent cell-mate when he noticed that Thomas was struggling to come to terms with yet another day.

'I must tell this boy now!' was the immediate thought of the new convert. Then he procrastinated.

'It will be better when I am out on the floor, and dressed,' he decided.

That was to prove a misjudgment.

What Thomas had momentarily forgotten was that Jim was an orderly. And he was on the first shift in the morning. This meant that he was expected to present himself in the dining-room half-an-hour before the other prisoners to set the tables and help prepare the breakfast.

As Thomas footled about in his cell, busying himself doing very little, with Jim and he dodging each other in the confined space, he was wondering just how to tell Jim the good news, when the door clanked open.

"Ready, Jim?" a prison officer called in.

"Right, hold on, I'm coming!" was the duty orderly's instant response. And in five seconds he was away!

There was a hollow bang as the cell door was slammed shut behind him.

Jim was gone! And Thomas hadn't told him!

He stood staring, open-mouthed, at the back of the door.

The opportunity had been missed. And he had promised himself that he would tell Jim first, for after all, Jim was half-way to knowing already. Or so he said!

'Well, if I couldn't tell my mate,' he reasoned, 'I will go out into the corridor there, and tell some of the other boys.'

His little 'Let Him In!' booklet had recommended that perhaps he should 'confide in some other Christian first'. That would possibly be a good idea. There would be some of his Christian friends and caring counsellors passing by his door, he knew.

So, when he was dressed, Thomas planted himself, like Mr. Plod the Policeman, plonk in the middle of the eight foot wide corridor, just outside his cell. All the prisoners, either on the way to or from the canteen or the washroom had to pass him at that point. Standing there with feet set stiffly astride, and a satisfied smile on his face, Thomas tried to intercept some members of the passing stream.

Holding an arm out at either side of him, with the distinct appearance of somebody expecting something significant to happen, without being quite sure what it was, he greeted all the early-morning protest-block pedestrians.

"Morning, boys," he would say to a group of them, as they hurried briskly along. "I just want to..."

"Mornin' Tom!" they would respond chirpily. And sliding sideways past him, continue on their merry way.

There were even three Christians who passed him individually. On each occasion Thomas had made a half-hearted attempt to stop them with a weakly-waving arm, and a half-hearted attempt to tell them in a weakly-wavering voice.

"Morning Joe...or Sammy...or Billy," he would begin. "I would like to..."

"Mornin' Tom!" each one had retorted heartily. Then he invariably carried on past about his business, either to eat or to wash. Or maybe even to slop out.

Thomas was frustrated.

This was without doubt the most exciting morning of his life to date.

He felt happier than he had ever been in his life to date.

And he couldn't even manage to tell anybody about it!

Then he remembered Bobby, who was in the cell at the very end of the corridor. Bobby was a Christian but Thomas hadn't seen him in the careering corridor crowd. If he was still in his dead-end cell the stymied new convert could corner him there and tell him the wonderful news. He was sure Bobby would be delighted.

On choosing to negotiate the length of the corridor, against the oncoming tide, Thomas was hailed by many more moving-forward-firmly 'Mornin' Tom!' mates.

When he at length arrived at Bobby's cell and peered in it was only to find that Bobby, whom he was intending to tell, Bobby who would doubtless be delighted, was sound asleep!

He looked so comfortable, too, all curled up in his bunk!

Thomas decided that it would be unfair to wake him up. 'Maybe he is very tired,' he thought, 'and if I rouse he may not just accept my news as eagerly as I had anticipated.'

Having stood there dithering for two or three minutes, listening to Bobby grunting and groaning, and watching him tossing and turning in his sleep, Thomas turned reluctantly away.

It would be most unfair to disturb him.

As he shuffled back towards his own cell Thomas felt a bit of a failure. He had let himself, or perhaps it was God, down, he reckoned.

Yes, he was saved.

And yes, he was glad he was saved.

Why then could he not summon up enough courage, or find the right words to tell even somebody about it?

Last night he had just been going to tell everybody!

Up until that moment, though, he hadn't even succeeded in telling anybody!

'Could it be that you just imagined it all last night?' disturbing doubts began to suggest. 'You are nothing but another phoney. You have made the whole thing up. Perhaps Jesus hasn't come into your life at all!'

The sense of purpose and ultimate fulfilment in his heart and soul convinced the new convert in a very short time, however, that he could, and should, banish all such misgivings from his mind. Once and for all. And for ever.

He just had to tell someone of his salvation soon.

But WHO?

19

'YOU HAVE WHAT?!'

Then it dawned on him. When he realized that there was a simple and obvious solution to his problem, Thomas wondered why he hadn't thought of it long ago!

He would tell his brother David. Thomas remembered, and he was sure David would remember, too, the night when their father had called his boys up to his bedroom, for he had 'something to tell' them.

Now he had 'something to tell' his brother.

Out in the busy corridor Thomas could mysteriously find the words, and the courage, to ask some of the prisoner passers-by, "Hi boys, have any of you seen my brother Davy this morning?"

"Aye, I have indeed Tom," one of an accosted group volunteered. "I saw him just a minute or two ago. He was heading up to the washroom."

Taking time only to utter a hasty, "Thanks, lads!" Thomas set off at double-quick speed, leaving three bemused men on their way to breakfast standing confused in the corridor.

'Tom' certainly was in some hurry today! And at that time of the morning too! Something big must have happened to the Martins!

Having dashed down to his own cell to pick up his wash gear he set off again. Although Thomas was fussy enough about personal hygiene he never usually ran to the washroom, but he did that morning. He knew he had to catch David before he got to breakfast. And he did.

Most of the other men had already washed and were gone, so Thomas found his brother in the washroom with an entire row of cockroach-free washbasins all to himself. David was using one of the middle basins, and Thomas, with almost the whole block to choose from, set his toilet bag down on the basin right beside him.

David was brushing his teeth. Frothy bubbles of father-furnished toothpaste were making their escape from the corners of his mouth.

Thomas turned on a tap at his washbasin, with a lot more deliberate thought than the turning on of a tap would normally require. Then he turned it off again, slowly, thoughtfully.

This was it. His big chance. He and his brother, side by side.

Turning sharply, suddenly, perhaps even somewhat nervously, Thomas seized his opportunity.

"Davy, I have something to tell you," he began.

"And what is that, Tom?" the younger brother asked, his mouth still full of toothbrush, and his words muffled, almost incoherent.

"I have become a Christian," Thomas informed him in one bold but brief announcement.

Brother David stopped brushing. He removed the toothbrush and held it poised stiffly before him like a orchestral conductor's baton, before exclaiming, in excitement rather than disdain, "You have *WHAT*?!"

At last the ice was broken. Thomas had actually managed to tell somebody. He began to feel better at once. But now there was no going back.

"I have just told you, Davy, I have got saved. Last night in my cell, lying in my bunk, reading a wee book one of the boys gave me, I asked Jesus to come into my heart," he went on to elaborate, for the benefit of his brother, who was obviously pleased. Perhaps even to the extent of being delighted. He had known that 'Tom' was spending a lot of his spare time with the Christian guys, and that didn't annoy him, for deep down he respected them himself. And he had a feeling that something like this was coming.

"Have you told anybody else about this, Tom?" he enquired enthusiastically.

"No, I haven't told another soul yet," Thomas replied. "I thought I would tell you first." What he did not dare confess to his brother that he had previously spent all of fifteen minutes trying to tell some of the other prisoners, but had failed miserably to do so!

"Well, we will soon tell somebody!" was David's instant reaction. By this time the strangely proud younger brother had zipped up his soap-bag, had thrown his towel carelessly across his arm, and was striding purposefully out of the washroom, to the buzz of the corridor beyond. He left behind him his newly converted, and having-now-confessed-his-faith, brother 'Tom', to continue his ablutions, contain his elation, and await developments.

Although David was not a Christian himself, he had come into contact with Christianity at close quarters in a marvellously altered, wonderfully attentive, father, and he knew how potentially life-transforming this news of his older brother's conversion could prove to be. So as Thomas proceeded with his morning wash he could hear David proclaiming the 'good news', as he made his way back along towards his cell.

"Did you hear the latest?" he would stop groups of prisoners and ask, the excitement in his voice and the sparkle in his eye compelling them to pay immediate attention. David wasn't going to settle for any, 'Mornin' Davy-but-we're-in-a-hurry half-hearted slide-on-by response.

"No. What's the latest?" one of the fairly-puzzled fellow-prisoners was sure to enquire.

"It's our Tom! He became a Christian last night! He has got saved, he says!" David was happy to let them know.

The news spread like wildfire.

Soon everybody on the wing, prisoners and duty prison officers alike, had heard about 'Tom' Martin's experience of the night before, and his confession to brother David that morning.

It wasn't long until some of the other Christians, who had witnessed to him so often, and who had now seen their 'And what about yourself, Tom?' question, answered, were out looking for Thomas.

And before he left the washroom two of them found him there.

When they told him that they had just heard 'great news', the recent convert was afforded another opportunity to confess his faith in Christ, and that is exactly what he did, telling them simply how he had opened his heart to let Jesus come in, the previous night.

As he continued to describe that wonderful experience to those two thrilled Christian men, Thomas felt an indescribable sense of joy and contentment flood over his soul. The hard, cold tiled floor of the washroom felt like an expensive, soft and warm Axminster carpet with a six-inch pile, to him. He was walking on air. And talking of peace.

The realization that his sin, and all of his sin, had been forgiven the moment he accepted the Saviour, he almost found impossible to comprehend. But he did believe it and it left him so overjoyed that he wanted to laugh and cry, run around and sit still, shout out and stay silent, all at once!

It was a wonderful, inexpressible sensation!

He was saved. He knew he was saved.

And nobody would ever make him doubt it again!

By the time he had finished speaking to his friends in the washroom people were looking for him all over the block. They wanted to congratulate him, to wish him 'every blessing', to let him know that they respected his courage, and some of them even assured him that they would 'be praying for' him.

All that day, that soul-thrilling Tuesday, Thomas Martin basked in the glow of his newly-found faith. Having told others of his commitment to Christ he began gradually to appreciate the riches that were his, 'in Christ Jesus'. And the greatest of these was the sensation that he had first felt the previous evening, that though still physically a prisoner he was spiritually free.

One of the other Christian prisoners had, at some stage during that ecstatic day, quoted a verse from the Bible to him, and it just described exactly how he felt. It was, his friend had said, from John chapter eight, and the words were, 'If the Son therefore shall make you free, you shall be free indeed.'

It was those last two words particularly that expressed his condition so precisely. Never before had he felt so 'free indeed'. He was liberated, emancipated, and relishing every moment of his new life in Christ, as a child of God and the son of a King.

After lock up that evening Thomas commandeered the cell's sole table and chair. He had two things left to do before he retired for the night after his first full day as a Christian.

The first of those two matters requiring his attention concerned his cell-mate, Jim. He was now in a position to do something he had been thwarted from doing both the night before, and that very morning. Telling him that he had become a Christian.

Looking across from the table to where Jim was relaxing on his bottom bunk, reading and smoking, Thomas broached the subject.

"Jim, do you remember what you said to me last night?" he asked.

"Yes, I do Tom, and some of the other boys have told me it has happened," Jim replied with a knowing smile.

"I was saved lying up there while I was reading that little book, and just after you went to sleep," Thomas went on to put him in the picture. Although 'some of the other boys had already told him', Thomas considered it important that he should also witness to his cell-mate himself.

'That's good, Tom. That's good," Jim replied. And then he went on, with a mischievous, almost childish expression, "I told you that was going to happen. Now didn't I?"

"Yes Jim, you did. You did," Thomas had to admit, but by that time Jim had his book up over his face again. The subject was obviously closed for now.

Undeterred, Thomas returned to the other job he had on hand.

He was writing a letter.

To his father.

20

ON TOP OF THE POPS

The words just flowed from his overflowing heart, through his happy head and his poised pen, on to the waiting paper.

Thomas was describing to his father, as graphically as possible, what had happened the previous evening. And how that Tommy Martin's fervent prayers for his sons had begun to be answered. The first of them had come to know the Saviour, in whom he himself had trusted, seven years before.

How thrilling! In addition to that wonderful answer to prayer in his salvation Thomas thought it would also be of particular interest to their caring, praying father to learn that it was actually David who had been proudly proclaiming the news of his older brother's conversion throughout the prison!

When at last he had finished that lengthy letter Thomas read it all over again, and as he did so, he felt himself all welling up inside. Tears weren't far away. And if he felt like weeping what would his father not be like when he received that letter in a few day's time?

It was great. Thomas was 'on top of the world' all through the next day. He spoke fearlessly to all of his friends in the prison, telling of his experience of salvation on Monday night.

On Thursday though, came the first real test of his faith. And his commitment to Christ, and the things of God.

It came when he found himself confronted with a choice.

One of the most popular TV programmes of the week in the Maze, 'Top of The Pops', was screened every Thursday evening at seven o'clock. Many of the prison inmates were fans of rock and pop, and hence seats were always at a premium for that programme.

Throughout his teenage years Thomas Martin had been one of those avid pop music followers, and now that he was in his early twenties nothing had changed. He was invariably amongst the first to be down in the canteen for the Thursday evening show. To him 'Top Of The Pops' was the can't-miss-must-see programme of the week. And had been for years. He followed closely the music, and to perhaps a lesser extent the fame and fortune, of such groups as Eurythmics and UB40, and pop idols like David Bowie.

Thomas knew them all. He had read it all up in the pop music magazines.

Now, however, he was a Christian.

So now, too, he had a difficult decision to make, for the only meeting of the Christian group which he had not as yet attended was the Thursday evening Bible study which was held at the same time as his favourite programme. Thomas had always been in the canteen, glued to the screen, at that particular time.

At breakfast time on the Thursday morning, Bobby, the sleeping Christian of Tuesday morning, unwittingly stuck Thomas right up on the horns of a dilemma.

"Would you like to come along to our Bible study group this evening, Tom?" he invited his friend, warmly. "I'm sure you would find it helpful. We are reading a book by Dr. Martyn Lloyd-Jones and discussing it together at the minute."

"Thanks for the invitation, Bobby," Thomas hedged, "but I don't think I will be able to make it this evening,"

"Oh that's O.K. Don't worry about it, Tom," Bobby replied sympathetically, probably realizing the reason and sensing the struggle in the new Christian's soul. "Any time you feel like it just come along. We will always be glad to see you."

It was left at that.

'Come when you like. We will always be glad to see you.'

Thomas now had a calculated choice to make.

Should he join the Christians in their Bible study? Or should he simply take his place before the TV screen as usual for 'Top Of The Pops'?

All day he wrestled with it.

He had told Bobby that he probably wouldn't 'make it' to the Bible study that evening and ever since he had said that he hadn't been happy. Not for a minute. His euphoria had evaporated. His conscience had been pricked.

What Thomas didn't realize during those hours of mental and spiritual turmoil was that he now had a new nature implanted within him. And this new nature wanted to go to the Bible study!

As the afternoon wore on Thomas knew that he had to come to some conclusion. Make some decision. Do something.

It was a battle, but before teatime he had made his choice, and after tea, when he saw three Christians going past his cell on the way to the Bible study, Thomas fell into step about twenty yards behind them.

On reaching the cell where the study was to be held the three men entered and pushed the door half-shut behind them, as though expecting others to arrive.

And another did arrive.

Thomas Martin approached the half-shut door and pushing it wide open, walked in.

"Excuse me, boys," he began, almost apologetically. "Would it be all right if I came to your meeting?"

"No problem. Come on over here and find yourself somewhere to sit," one of the men already seated on the bottom bunk called out.

"It's great to see you, Tom," another said, with genuine warmth and enthusiasm. "Of course it's all right for you to join us!"

So Thomas sat down in the most inconspicuous spot he could find and then spent almost two hours with those Christian prisoners as they read and discussed the book by Dr. Martyn Lloyd-Jones that

Bobby had told him about that morning. The book was about the problems of spiritual depression, and since they had plenty of time every Scripture reference was turned up, read out, and duly discussed.

It was all so new. So stimulating. So exciting for Thomas. Although he didn't understand a quarter of what the men were talking about for at least half of the time Thomas found the bits that he did understand quite inspiring. And although he had always felt secure in the presence of this Christian group before, he now felt even more at home.

He sensed that he was wanted there now because he actually **belonged** there.

Thomas was one of them, in every sense of the word.

Meanwhile, back in the canteen, eyebrows were being raised, and questions were being asked.

'Tom' Martin's seat was empty.

"Where's Tom?" one or two enquired. "Is he not coming down tonight?"

"No, I wouldn't think so," somebody else who considered himself well up in such matters, retorted. "He has 'seen the light' you know. He will likely be at that Bible study thing them Christian boys run every Thursday night."

And he was right.

'Tom' was 'at that Bible study thing'.

He had made a deliberate decision.

With the help of the Spirit of God he had got on top of the pops. He had overcome them. Conquered them. Put them behind him.

And he never went back to the canteen at seven o'clock on a Thursday night.

Never, ever, again.

21

HALLELOOOOOJAH!

It was early Sunday morning in the prison and Thomas lay on his top bunk with his hands behind his head. The cell door had been opened and he was at that moment deciding whether or not to get up. And then, having concluded that it was probably time to rise, he began to direct his mind to another decision he had to make.

Would he wash first? Or have breakfast first?

Some days he did it one way. Some days another.

By the time he had swung his legs over the edge of his bunk he had made up his mind. He reached for his towel. It would be wash, then eat, that day.

Outside in the corridor the muffled routine of morning continued as it did at the start of every day.

There was the shuffle of feet as coming-awake men began to move about.

From the washroom came the sound of running water and mumbled greetings.

Suddenly the shadowy stillness was split wide open by a short sharp shout.

"Halleloooooojah!"

The exclamation was sufficiently loud, and held in its central syllable sufficiently long, so that everybody on the wing could hear.

Thomas jettisoned his towel and sprang to the floor.

"I guarantee you that's our David!" he said, but only to himself, for cell-mate Jim had long-since gone. "Dave has been asking a lot of questions, and showing a lot of interest in spiritual matters recently."

Thomas had spoken to his brother about salvation almost every day since his own conversion, and he had certainly prayed for him earnestly every night, and usually often during the day as well

It just had to be David!

And he was right. It was!

When he had hit the floor Thomas catapulted himself across to the door in one huge bound. Then, on peering out into the corridor, he was thrilled at what he saw.

David was coming along, approaching his big brother's cell, with his face shining. Jim Watt had his arm around his shoulder.

It had been to Jim, about five minutes earlier, that David had first dared to confess his faith in Christ. Very quietly. Very nervously.

It was July 31st, 1983, and David had been saved in his cell in the early hours of that morning. When he had ventured out into the corridor, determined to tell someone about it, as soon as possible, Jim had been the first Christian he had spotted, walking just ahead of him. On quickening his pace David had drawn up alongside him and whispered, "I thought you would like to know, I got saved last night, Jim."

Looking across at the blushing, but beaming, younger man, Jim retorted, "What's that, Davy?" pretending not to hear.

"I said, I got saved last night, Jim," David repeated, slightly louder.

"Say that again, Davy. What was that?" Jim persisted, cupping his hand to his ear and feigning deafness.

"What I am trying to tell you is, I got saved last night!" David repeated once more, but by then he was becoming exasperated, for by then he was almost shouting.

That had been Jim's ultimate intention all along. To make this babe in Christ proclaim his newly-found faith so boldly that others all around would hear. There could be no place for half-hearted, back-door, Sundays-only, secret disciples in prison.

And when he was eventually satisfied with both the volume, and the sincerity of David's confession of salvation, it had been Jim who had bellowed the resounding "Halleloooooojah!" which had launched Thomas into action.

As they approached the door where Thomas was standing, mesmerized, immobile, Jim withdrew his arm from David's shoulder and stopped. Then he pushed the new convert forward, ahead of him.

"Go on, Davy," he urged. "Tell Tom the good news."

David dropped his head for a second, then lifting his eyes to catch those of his expectant brother, he said simply, "Tom, I just want to tell you that I got saved last night in my cell."

Overcome with emotion, Thomas just reached forward and put his arms around 'young Davy'. They hugged each other warmly. Blood brothers who had once been partners in crime, had become fellow-prisoners, and were now fellow-Christians, children of God, and joint-heirs with Jesus!

No wonder they felt like celebrating!

Tears flowed.

Thomas punctuated the joyful, tearful silence periodically with a powerful, "Praise the Lord!"

Not to be left out, and anxious to be seen to be part of this impromptu, on the landing, praise service, Jim Watt forced a way in between the two exultant brothers, and soon there were three of them, locked at the shoulders, heads bowed towards the centre, jigging about. Calling out. Praising God.

Other prisoners passed by on the other side.

Many of them looked cynically on all this emotionalism. They had become wary of all these Christians and their 'witness', as they called it. Acutely aware that there was a code of honesty with this 'Christianity' they were frightened that some of these men would take their newly-embraced upright-living too far, and turn supergrass, incriminating some of them.

David and Thomas Martin didn't care what they thought, though. They knew they were happy. And they knew somebody else who would be happy, too.

Their father, Tommy.

On Tuesday morning, Tommy Martin received another thrilling letter. From David this time. The one which he had received in mid-June from Thomas had given him untold joy, and he had thanked God whole-heartedly for such a wonderful answer to prayer. But that had only been fifty per cent of his prayers for his 'boys in prison' answered, and from then on he had prayed all the more fervently for David.

Now those prayers had been answered also.

On the morning he received that letter from his second son to be saved Tommy sat back in his armchair, tears of joy glistening on his haggard cheeks.

He smiled ruefully to himself as he reflected on how he used to inform Thomas so sincerely that he believed the Lord had a purpose in he and David being in prison. And how mad Thomas used to become at that!

Now that prediction had proved correct.

A scripture verse, from the short letter which Paul had written to Philemon about his runaway slave, Onesimus, flashed into his mind again. He had often gleaned solace from those words in recent difficult times. Through the on-the-stepthrough-in-the-snow long dark winter days, or during the lonely, wakeful, seemingly endless, long dark winter nights they had been a constant source of encouragement and an unextinguished, though often spluttering, beacon of hope to him.

He reached across to the table beside him and lifted his well-worn Bible. It didn't take him long to find his verse, either. He had a marker in the page.

Tommy was one of those people who appreciated the impact of print better if he read it aloud. So he read his own, Tommy-Martinmodified-version of the verse aloud, softly. Over, and over again...

'For perhaps *they* therefore departed for a season, that thou shouldest receive *them* forever...

For perhaps *they* therefore departed for a season that thou shouldest receive *them* forever...

For perhaps *they* therefore departed for a season ...'

It was so true.

Both of Tommy's sons had departed for a season. For a relatively lengthy prison term, in fact.

But now they would be with him, forever. For the rest of their lives, whether in or out of prison. And also through the endless eons of eternity, in heaven.

He closed his Bible and placed it tenderly back on the table.

Then he dried his eyes with the sleeve of his pullover and whispered softly, "Thank you! Thank you! Thank you, Lord!"

22

'GOD HAD SHUT THE LIONS' MOUTHS, SO THEY COULD NOT HARM HIM'

It was exciting. Absolutely thrilling.

As they revelled together, and individually, through personal and collective prayer and Bible study, in their new-every-morning discoveries of their privileges and responsibilities as Christians, Thomas and David were drawn closer to God. And also to each other.

Thomas gradually came down to earth from his post-conversion out-of-this-world walking-on-air experience, followed by the euphoria of David's salvation. As summer rolled on into autumn he became reconciled once more to the hum-drum routine of the prison. Now, though, he had something, and Somebody, more to live for.

Old things, and old desires, had passed away.

All things had become new.

Then, in late November, 1983, he and his younger brother had a strange spiritual experience.

One morning David came out of his cell and made his way along to see his brother, before breakfast. He had something urgent he must tell Thomas. And although they had all of that day, and hundreds of others, stretching out ahead of them, it definitely could not be left until later on!

"I know it is kind of early in the day, Tom," he began half-apologetically, when they met, "but I have something I feel I need to share with you, and I felt I ought to do it as soon as possible."

Thomas was dumbfounded.

"Funny you should say that, Davy," he replied, when he had overcome the initial shock, "for I was just on my way out to try to find you! There is something that I feel I need to share with YOU!"

For weeks God had been speaking to Thomas, telling him to leave the protest wing. It wasn't right. It wasn't Christian. And he should not be part of it.

Although this conviction had grown stronger with every passing day, Thomas had endeavoured, unsuccessfully to drive it to the back of his mind. He hoped that it would eventually burn itself out, and blow away. But it didn't.

The new Christian was scared of what God was trying to tell him, for he was well aware of what the consequences of it could mean. If he came 'off the protest' he was sure he would be branded a coward, a 'chicken', a traitor. Or worse. And that was not to mention what reprisals, what punishments, what 'measures', could be taken against him physically.

It didn't even bear contemplation.

Thomas was curious to find out what it was that David so much wanted to tell him. Could it possibly be anything to do with...?

"Go ahead, Davy," he invited, "You go first. What's on you mind?"

"It's just this, Tom," David began to explain. "Last night in my cell I was reading the Bible in Second Corinthians chapter six and I came upon this verse which said, 'Come out from among them, and be ye separate, saith the Lord, and touch not the unclean thing ; and I will receive you.'

When he paused for a moment, Thomas began to anticipate his next sentence. And when he heard it, he had been correct. He could feel the goose-pimples rising all over his body, and began to sense the shivers running down his spine as David continued, "I have hardly slept a wink all night, Tom, thinking about this, for I believe God wants us to leave the protest."

Thomas was stunned.

"Do you know what I was about to tell you?" he asked, a tremble creeping into his voice. "I was going to try to find you to tell you that last night I was reading the Bible too, but I was reading in Matthew chapter six, and I couldn't get past one of the verses in there. This is what it says, 'No man can serve two masters : for either he will hate the one, and love the other ; or else he will hold to the one, and despise the other. Ye cannot serve God and mammon.'

That's what I have been trying to do for this past four or five months, Davy," he went on to tell his brother of his concern. "I have been trying to serve two masters. These boys in here, on the wing. And God. And the Bible says it can't be done!"

He looked upset.

"Just as a matter of interest," David digressed for a minute, for something had just stuck him that might be significant, and he needed it clarified, "what time were you doing your reading at last night, Tom?"

"Oh, I suppose it was sometime between half-nine and ten," Thomas replied, "Why?"

"Because it was sometime between half-nine and ten that I was doing my reading, too," David retorted, his voice fading away in silent wonder. His face was a picture.

The two brothers stood staring at each other. They were in a state of spiritual shock.

"Do you know what this means, Tom?" it was David who resumed the conversation. "It means that God is speaking to the both of us. And we are going to have to do something about it!"

"Yes, you are probably right, Davy," Thomas replied, thoughtfully. "But what? What are we going to do?" He did not for one minute fancy the prospect of telling some of these hardened protesters, and especially the wing commanders, that he was leaving. Had just decided to 'pack it in'.

"We will have to get off the protest, Tom," he suggested tentatively, timorously. The thought of the stand they were going to have to take didn't altogether send him into ecstasies, either.

They both decided, however, that difficult though it would be, God had spoken clearly to each of them, by different verses, in different cells, but at around the same time, and they had no choice but to listen.

It was His Word. It was His way. It was His will.

And it would have to be done.

When the two brothers had devised, then discarded, a number of different plans, discussed dozens of different ways of saying exactly the same thing, and spent a few more separate, but sleepless, nights in practically-panicking prayer, they decided that they were as ready as they would ever be to approach the wing commanders.

One afternoon, just after two o'clock, when all the prisoners had been let out for recreation, Thomas and David spoke to Billy in the corridor. By then they were both absolutely shaking in their shoes. This could be an extremely dicey thing to do.

"I say Billy, could Davy and I have a wee word with you and maybe a couple of the other commanders?" Thomas asked, struggling manfully to keep his voice from shaking.

"Certainly, Tom, no problem," Billy responded cheerily. "Come on back to my room where we can have a chat."

When they had returned to Billy's room, having invited two other loyalist leaders on the wing, to join them on the way, the three commanders were curious to know what was on the Martin minds. 'Tom' and 'Davy' never gave any trouble and it was strange that they should request a meeting. There must be something big going on.

"Well, boys, what can we do for you? What's your problem?" Billy enquired, acting as spokesman for 'the management'.

"It's just like this," Thomas, the older of the two brothers, and their opening spokesman, began uneasily, "we want to leave the protest."

The three commanders looked shocked, and Billy, who had heard requests like this before, jumped to an instant, but inaccurate, conclusion, as to why two men who had once been so militant, would want to 'chicken out'.

"What's wrong, Tom, is there somebody bothering you?" he wanted to know. "Is there somebody giving you a hard time?

Somebody on your back like? Don't worry about it. You tell us and we will sort it out, believe me!"

Standing there before those three hard, tough, loyalist leaders, to take their stand for what they believed, David and Thomas Martin didn't feel like some big heroes for the faith. They were just scared stiff. For if this all turned sour they could be left permanently scarred.

It was dreadful beyond description.

"No, Billy, it's nothing like that," Thomas went on talking while David beside him went on praying.

"Well what is the problem then?" Billy and the other two commanders were anxious to ascertain.

"The problem is that we are Christians now," Thomas explained, gradually growing in a confidence which could only have come from God. "And as Christians we feel it is not right for us to be on the protest. We should be conforming to prison regulations. You see we have a new Commander in our lives now. We want to serve God."

What a statement! To three of the most influential loyalist leaders in the Maze!

There followed a brief consultation between the wing commanders, two of whom were UVF men and the third was from the UDA. These were men with fixed fanatical ideals and few scruples.

How would it go?

Thomas and David dreaded their decision. They were sure that it would, at least, involve some sort of reprisal for reneging on their commitment to 'the cause'.

It was a tense time.

The atmosphere was electric.

The two brothers drew breath in brief bursts.

When they had deliberated for the most of ten minutes the three leaders faced the two prisoners who had chosen to place themselves under new Command, again.

They were ready to deliver their verdict

Billy continued in his role as spokesman.

"We have been watching you boys for months," he informed them, "and we know that you are genuine, through and through. You probably don't realize it, either, but you have a tremendous calming influence on this wing. We don't want to lose you. We will do anything to help the pair of you, just to keep you. Would you not consider changing your mind?"

David and Thomas could barely believe what they were hearing.

When he had recovered his composure Thomas also recovered his voice.

"Thank you for saying that Billy, but we are definitely going. The Lord is our Commander now, and this is a big thing for us", he told them, with a strange mixture of relief tinged with regret.

"Well if that's the way you feel about it, then you may go," Billy conceded to a slow nodding of heads from the other two. He then added, with a grudging respect, "We have to say that we appreciate the fact that you have come to tell us that you were leaving. At least you didn't go squealing to the Governor and then 'squeaky booting it out' in the middle of the night."

Just as he had finished speaking the other two men, Jim, and a second Billy, stepped forward and shook hands with 'Tom' first, and then 'Davy'. Billy, the spokesman, followed suit.

As the two Christian prisoners crossed towards the door, and were about to leave the room, and the 'interview', Billy called after them, "And you can be sure, boys, that nobody will say anything to you. And nobody will do anything to you. Just leave that with us!"

Thomas felt weak as he walked out towards the exercise yard. He looked across at the dumbfounded David. The colour was slowly beginning to return to young brother's once-white cheeks.

They both felt enveloped by an uncanny sense of calm.

The minds which had once been paralyzed with fear and dread were now relaxed in peace and joy.

Neither spoke.

It was just incredible!

Thomas smiled comfortably to himself. Words began to repeat themselves, drumming over and over in his mind. They were part of a chorus he had learnt many years before in the C.E. in Lurgan. Thanks, again, of course, to the enterprising Elsie.

The chorus was all about Daniel in 'the den of lions', and it ended with these words...

'In the den, in the den,
Fears could not alarm him,
God had shut the lions' mouths,
So they could not harm him.'
It was so true. And it described precisely how he felt.

David and he had just been released, unscathed. From a 'den of lions', who could easily have made mincemeat of the both of them!

But 'God had shut the lions' mouths,
So they could not harm' them.

And next day they were allowed to 'leave the protest', and were transferred back to one of the 'conforming' wings of the Maze.

23

PENPAL

Meanwhile, life 'beyond the wire' continued as normal, and there were some people on 'the outside' who had developed a genuine interest in the welfare of the prisoners. And particularly the Christian prisoners. One such person was Florence Cobb, whose husband had been killed in a terrorist attack. Rather than spend the remainder of her life in lonely and bitter isolation, however, Florence had established a contact ministry with Christians in prison. And it was she who had given the name of a prisoner 'who would like to receive a letter from a Christian girl', to Gaye Matthews.

Soon Gaye began her first letter. It was difficult to know exactly what to write to somebody you had never met before in your life! And him in prison, too! Gaye had no idea what sort of a character this Jim 'Hovis' Brown was, but she had been assured that he was a Christian, and she was a Christian also, that was always a starting point.

During the morning-break one day, in the shop where she worked in Lisburn, Gaye had her pen and writing-pad out again. She had thought of a few more sentences to write. Another piece of relatively trivial news which she thought might be of interest to this Jim, whoever he was.

Another shop assistant noticed her friend, who was usually just bubbling over with chat at the morning tea break about what had happened the night before, and what was going to happen that night she hoped, totally absorbed in her letter writing.

"What are you doing, Gaye?" she enquired, puzzled.

"A woman gave me the name of a boy in prison. She gets people to write letters to Christian prisoners. So that's what I am doing, June, I am trying to write a letter to some body I never met in my life. I don't know what he looks like, don't know where he comes from, don't even know what age he is! All I know is that he is called Jim Brown," Gaye replied, with a short laugh. When she had finished her explanation the whole idea had sounded a bit daft!

Then Gaye had an idea. She knew that her work-mate was a Christian as well so she pushed the writing-pad across to her and asked, "Here June, would you like to add a wee bit to the end of this letter?"

"Yes, I might as well," came the reply. Then she hesitated. "But what will I say?" she went on, with an embarrassed almost girlish giggle.

"Well you could tell him who you are for a start!" Gaye suggested.

So, sitting down beside Gaye, both of them squashed on to the one chair, she wrote her few introductory sentences.

'My name is June Thompson. I am praying for you, too. My address is 28, North Street, Upper Ballinderry.'

That was enough for a start, she thought, for she couldn't think of anything else sensible to write, which Gaye had not already written. She stood up, passed the writing-pad back to her friend, and promptly forgot all about it!

A few days later, in the Maze prison, Jim 'Hovis' Brown tracked Thomas down in the exercise yard. He had a letter flapping about in his hand.

"Hey Tom, how would you like to write out to a Christian girl?" he wanted to know, with a twinkle in his eye. "I have the names and addresses of two of them here, and one will probably be enough for me!"

Thomas thought about it for a minute.

"Yes, I suppose I would, Jim, it would always be something more to do," he concluded, after only brief reflection.

Jim then flattened out the flapping letter. It was now time to sort out the practicalities of this penpal issue.

"Which one of them do you want to write to?" Jim asked.

"And how would I know?!" Thomas laughed. "Which one actually wrote to you?"

"It was this girl Gaye Matthews," Jim replied after a brief glance at the letter.

"O.K. then, I will write to the other one," Thomas agreed. "What did you say her name is?" One was the same as the other to him, at that stage, for he was not likely to know either of them.

Jim took another dive into the letter.

"She is called June Thompson, and here is her address, " Jim volunteered, tearing off, and presenting to Thomas, a roughly ripped scrap of paper. It was June's three sentence contribution to what had been Gaye's laborious letter.

When he returned to his cell for lock-up that evening Thomas wrote a short letter of introduction to this June Thompson, whoever she was. He was now in Gaye's predicament of the previous week. What do you say to somebody you don't even know?!

It was early November, 1985, and almost two years had elapsed since the simultaneous revelations to David and himself, and 'coming off the protest'. Thomas had made slow but steady spiritual growth in that time, and he related to his new Christian penpal the story of how he had come to know the Lord in prison. And what had happened since, as well.

When he had written a couple of pages Thomas decided to stop. What was the point in writing too much? The girl from Upper Ballinderry might not even get the letter, and even if she did what would she care about him? She might not even bother to reply. She might have a boy-friend of her own who wouldn't like her writing to another man. And a paramilitary prisoner to boot!

He would wait and see!

On Thursday 7th November, June Thompson was surprised to find, on returning home from work, that there was a letter for her. She didn't normally receive a lot a personal mail, and she certainly had never received a letter like this one before, for it had the Maze Prison censorship stamp on it. Twice.

So somebody had written to her! From prison!

June was more pleased than she cared to admit with that letter. It gave her a glow of satisfaction inside. Somebody had cared enough about her, having had nothing more than her name and address, to write her a letter.

It also gave her a sense of purpose. Here was something profitable for a shy and unassuming Christian young woman to do,. She could write to a Christian in prison. It might be an encouragement to this Thomas chap, if she started to correspond with him. So she wrote back.

In about a week's time she received a reply.

Then she wrote back, again.

And in about a week's time she received yet another reply.

Gradually June and Thomas, who as yet had never met, built up a regular pattern of correspondence, with the interval between sending the letter and receiving a reply becoming ever shorter.

In early December Thomas received a Christmas card from June which he displayed proudly on the wall of his cell. It gave him a lot of pleasure.

Then, just two days before Christmas he received another card and this one became even more precious to him. On the outside of this second card the words 'THINKING OF YOU' were emblazoned in block capitals. Even more meaningful though, than the message on the outside was the hand-written inscription on the inside, for his new 'penpal' had written these words, 'I saw this card in the shop yesterday and I bought it for you for I thought you might be lonely at Christmas. I just wanted you to know that I AM thinking of you. June.'

That was enough to bring tears to a prisoner's eyes.

Tommy Martin had been very faithful to his son over his past four years in prison.

God, too, had kept the promise Thomas had discovered in the Bible one day. He had promised 'never to leave him or forsake him.'

Now here was somebody else whom he honestly believed was thinking about him.

It was so reassuring.

In January the letters became longer and more frequent.

Thomas and June had begun to share brief bursts of Christian encouragement with each other. They were a kind of a stay-up-and keep-going pat-on-the- back thought for the day, about twice a week. And occasionally, too, as life didn't always come up roses for them any more than for anybody else, they found themselves sharing the disappointments and discouragements they had experienced, as well.

Thomas soon decided that it was time to take this relationship one step farther. In one of his new year letters he asked June the question that had been on his mind since the two-cards-before Christmas apparent interest. If I send you out a visiting pass would you come in here to meet me? Or would you find it all too embarrassing to be seen to associate with a man in prison?

For two days Thomas waited. On the third day he watched out for the mail. And on the fourth day after he had written the reply came.

'Of course. I would love to come and visit you,' was June's by-return-of-post response. There was something warm, something encouraging, too, about the little condition June had attached to her visit. 'And could you possibly make it for a Wednesday', she had added, 'for Wednesday is my day off.'

Without wasting any more time Thomas applied for a visiting pass, for a Wednesday, was granted it, and immediately sent it out to June, the Christian girl whom by now he had written to often, but had still never met, from Upper Ballinderry.

It was all arranged.

June Thompson was to meet Thomas Martin in the Maze on Wednesday 5th February, 1986, at 2.30 p.m. Their first date!

For nights in his cell Thomas lay in his bunk, staring up at the ceiling, which wasn't far away. He was making mental preparation for that meeting. His big concern was, What will I say? What will we talk about?

It would be a mistake, he knew, to appear too forward. On the other hand it wouldn't be a great idea to appear too backward either!

Nor did he want to sound overly sensible. Or overtly stupid.

It wasn't quite as bad as preparing for 'the den of lions', but he wouldn't have Davy's support in this one. He would be on his own this time!

Back in Upper Ballinderry June had a problem, too. Hers was not about what she should say, for June was naturally a very retiring person who didn't usually have a lot to say about anything, but her problem was more to do with dress than dialogue.

What should she wear?

She gossiped with Gaye about it dozens of times, without ever coming to any conclusion.

She opened her wardrobe, and then shut it again, hundreds of times, without ever coming to any conclusion.

She didn't want this Thomas, who had after all, been in prison for four years, to think that she was some old-fashioned old-maid. Nor, though, did she want to appear too way-out either.

It was hard to know.

However when the appointed day came Thomas had formulated his set of essential but general Christian-type questions, and June had eventually come to a decision as to what to wear, and 2.30 p.m. that afternoon was a momentous occasion for them both. Face to face at last!

Thomas did most of the talking, and at the first the conversation was understandably formal, stilted, nervous.

June smiled a lot, blushed a lot, answered her 'penpal's' questions about her work, her family, and her church, in short terse statements, but other than asking a couple of self-conscious questions about life in prison, she left the cues for conversation all to Thomas.

When the visit was over, and June had returned home after a bashful 'Goodbye', Thomas went back to his cell and wrote her a long letter. When complete it was by far the longest to date.

In it he told her how much he had appreciated her coming to see him, how much he had enjoyed the visit, and by far the most significant of all, how he 'really liked' her.

He had considered using the word 'love' somewhere in it, but then after much heart-rending heart-searching, decided against it.

Maybe it was just a wee bit too soon for that!

Perhaps 'love' would come later.

24

PICK IT UP AND PUT IT BACK!

Back on the 'conforming wings' of the prison Thomas and David Martin didn't want to waste their time. So much of their lives had already been devoted to pointless pursuits, they now had a lot to catch up on. They wanted to make sure that every day, every hour, and indeed every minute if possible, counted for their new Master. God had given them such peace and purpose in their lives they wanted to share it with all the other prisoners when they had the chance. And before it was too late.

Their problem was, though, how could they ever contact every single prisoner with the message of the Gospel?

Having considered the matter for a few weeks the two brothers devised a plan. They came to a conclusion. There was a way in which it could be done.

Step number one was for Thomas and David to apply to join the Chief Officer's work party. This would be an important step for them, for it would allow them to extend their scope, which would be absolutely essential if they were to fulfil their dream. Prisoners who were selected to work for the Chief Officer were designated as 'trustees', and as such were granted certain privileges. One of these concessions was that they were allowed to work outside the prison walls and another, the one that immediately appealed to the Martin brothers, was that they could be posted to work in any or every corner of the prison complex.

Not every prisoner who applied to be selected as a 'trustee' was appointed, however. Every application was scrupulously examined and wide-ranging and thorough checks, particularly amongst prison officers who were in day-to-day contact with the men, were carried out. It would be important to find out if somebody was applying for some sinister and ulterior motive. Like escape, for instance!

Thomas and his brother had gradually built up for themselves a very favourable reputation within the prison. From the moment they came off the protest, acknowledging that they were now under the supreme control of a new and heavenly Commander, the two men in their twenties began to obey, to 'the letter of the law', all the prison rules. Their behaviour was an example to many. Such was their standing in the Maze, that other prisoners, both Christian and non-Christian, and a few prison officers, had actually come to them in secret, seeking advice on spiritual matters.

When the question of their application to join the Governor's work party came up for consideration, all those consulted had no hesitation in giving David and Thomas a glowing recommendation.

One prison officer, who had frequent contact with the two candidates, remarked when consulted, "I would trust the Martins with my wages!" Quite a statement from a man who was constantly 'watching his own back', and who thought he had long-since learnt, from bitter experience, never to trust any prisoner with any thing, at any time, ever!

It came as no surprise to anybody, really, then, when Thomas and David were informed, within a matter of weeks, that they had been chosen to serve on the Chief Officer's work party. This selection was recognized by their fellow-prisoners and approved by the prison officers.

One very welcome benefit of this new appointment was that Thomas and David were now entitled to a higher wage. They were awarded, upon promotion, the sum of £2.56 per week! To be on the Chief Officer's work party afforded the two brothers something which was more immediately important to them than financial gain, though.

Apart from the practical consideration of slightly more spending money, more freedom to move about under supervision, and work to do to pass the hours between visits by father, longer letters from Upper Ballinderry, and prayer meetings and Bible study groups, Thomas recognized, in this new position of trust, an unrivalled opportunity to serve God. And to achieve his goal.

When he was sure that he had established himself in his new role, Thomas asked a senior prison officer for permission to place a Gospel tract in every cell that he and his work party had refurbished or repainted, before leaving it for the final time. The officer granted this permission, probably reasoning that if the leaving of a 'Gospel tract', whatever that was, in every cell, would help transform some of the awkward men under his care into agreeable men like the Martins, it could only be a positive step. It would certainly make his life a lot easier!

Thomas, however, now that he had been given permission to pursue his vision, was faced with one very down-to-earth problem.

How, where, or from whom, did he actually obtain the tracts? It was all very well to have the pure-minded well-intentioned genuinely-concerned objective of placing a tract in every cell in the prison. How did he go about procuring the hundreds, perhaps even thousands, of tracts he was going to need?

Thomas was in prison. He couldn't just pop into his local Christian bookshop, browse for an hour or so, and then in his own good time set off for home with a bagful of suitable material. June did her best to drip-feed her fired-up friend with some tracts in her letters, but this, unknown to Thomas, caused her some heart searching at the time. Since all the mail entering the prison was restricted by weight, did she put in a seventh tract to tip the scales to maximum-permitted, or did she include an extra page of newsy love-stuff? Quite a dilemma! And the solution differed, depending on the mood of the day!

This was only a 'drop in the ocean' though. Six, or on a spiritual-high-for-June week, seven, tracts per letter could never help Thomas and David come anywhere near their projected aim. They wanted to ensure that no prisoner ever left the Maze without being challenged by the claims of Christ, in written form, in his cell. And it seemed a mammoth task.

The problem of the supply of suitable booklets was solved one day, quite unexpectedly, in a conversation Thomas had with a prison officer.

This particular officer was complimenting Thomas on 'the stand he had taken' in witnessing for Christ in the prison, and as he began to walk away he rounded off the conversation with an offer.

"If there is ever anything I can do to help you Thomas, just let me know," he volunteered.

"Do you really mean that?" Thomas retorted so quickly that the officer found himself a bit taken aback.

"Yes, I do, I really mean it," he replied, wondering what was coming next. Surely a sensible man like Thomas Martin wasn't going to ask him to do something ridiculous. Or dangerous.

This offer was an answer to prayer to the would-be-tract-distributor. It was too good an opportunity to miss.

"Yes, there is something you can do for me," Thomas continued eagerly, words tripping over each other to tumble out of his mouth. "Is there any chance of you buying a load of tracts and bringing them in here to me? I will get my father to pay you for them. Davy and I want to leave a tract in every cell in this place."

"That's a good idea, Tom. I like it," the officer responded, thoughtfully, obviously contemplating whether the ban on 'trafficking' between officer and prisoner extended to Gospel tracts.

"Leave it with me," he went on after a brief reflection. "I am in total sympathy with what you are trying to do. I won't promise anything, but I will see what I can do."

Days passed, with no tracts. Thomas hadn't seen that particular officer again for quite a while. He must have gone on holiday. Or perhaps he had been moved to another wing. Perhaps he had decided against becoming involved with Thomas and his big ideas and was merely avoiding him.

Prisoners have lots of time to think, and all sorts of notions flitted through the eager active mind of Thomas the would-be-leaflet-leaver.

Then, when he had almost given up hope of obtaining a substantial number of tracts from any source, and had become reconciled to working with the limited supply he and Davy could receive in letters, Thomas was awakened by a rustle outside his cell door in the early hours of the morning. It was well after midnight and the prison had settled down for the night. All was still. And only prison officers on the prowl should have been awake.

The startled prisoner sat bolt upright, struggling to shake himself awake.

The he heard someone half-whisper, half-whistle, "Pssssssst!" through their teeth. It was a weird wake-up call, without using names or stating a message.

Suddenly, while Thomas was still in the where-am-I-and-what's-happening? early stage of wakening up, a hoard of tracts were propelled in batches of eight or ten at a time in below the door. They flapped and fluttered to rest in untidy mounds all over the floor of his cell.

Then, as quickly as it had all begun, it all ceased. The prison returned to its normal sleeping silence. But Thomas and David had been supplied with the materials to at least begin their task in earnest. They could see their aim being achieved. Sometime. Somehow.

And the 'how' was now up to them.

Time was short. The task was daunting, and would possibly be difficult. So they began straight-away.

Packing their tracts into a small shoebox, 'Tom and Davy', as they were known to the others, put their plan into action. Having obtained further permission from the Chief Officer they stowed their box of literature inside the big work-box which contained all the tools used every day for their work on cell repair. This box had to be checked by the duty officer after every shift, and a missing hammer or chisel caused great consternation and usually activated a search. No doubt such tools could prove invaluable to an enterprising would-be escapee.

'Tom's wee box' gradually became accepted as an integral part of the overall tool-kit. Some of the other men on the work party joked about it, but none of them ever complained about it. 'Tom and Davy' were held in high regard amongst them. They 'went over the top a bit about religion, sometimes' but 'they were nice guys who would do anything for you', nonetheless! was the general consensus.

When they had finished either re-painting or perhaps re-furnishing a cell, then Thomas or his brother, would take a tract from their box and leave it on the locker. For the incoming occupants.

All the prison officers knew that Thomas and David had permission to do this, and would even ask them, as they closed up a completed a cell, "Did you leave them one of your wee books, boys?"

How God had prepared the way for them within the prison became evident one day when a new officer joined the squad supervising the work party. It was one of the responsibilities of a duty officer to inspect every cell when the work was done to ensure that everything was satisfactory, and had been left safe, for a new batch of prisoners, who were moved around on the rota, from block to block. Or from cell to cell.

This most recent official decided to flaunt his authority. The work-party, waiting in the corridor for him to complete his routine inspection, were astounded to see him emerge, and with an unmistakable venom crumple up the Thomas tract, and fling it up the corridor.

"There is no need for that kind of stuff in there!" he shouted sharply, a sly, see-what-a-smart-boy-am-I smile on his sneering face.

The senior prison officer, the person with ultimate charge over the work-party, was two cells ahead, carrying out another inspection. Alerted by the chorus of angry protest from the men in the corridor he returned immediately to find out for himself exactly what was going on. And it didn't take him long to discover the reason for their unrest, either, for every man seemed to have his eyes focussed on the screwed up tract where it lay tucked in a pathetic ball, in against the corridor wall.

"Here! You!" he called to the junior officer. "Come here this minute and pick that up and put it back where you found it! And don't you dare ever throw one of those wee books out again! These boys have permission to leave them in every cell, and they stay. Understand?!"

The smirk disappeared. The junior's face reddened. He stooped down, picked up the crushed tract, smoothed it out as best he could between his two hands, and then proceeded to do as he was told. Like a chastened schoolboy he retraced his steps into the still-open cell and replaced the still-creased tract on the exact spot from which he had lifted it, so defiantly, five minutes before.

The junior had got the message.

The principle was by now well established.

And the vision was well on its way to fruition.

25

OXOXOXOXOXOXOXO!

Thomas Martin had another matter on his mind those days in addition to his evangelical emphasis. His tract in a cell work-party pattern.

This second concern was perhaps more one of the heart than of the mind.

It was all to do with June.

From the hour of that first visit in February, 1986, Thomas had wanted to be more definite about June's feelings towards him. He was certainly in no doubt about his own feelings for her.

'Love' was the word he now used to describe to himself how he felt towards the shy girl from Upper Ballinderry who communicated with him by long letters when they were apart, and in short sentences when they were together. The big question was, though, did she feel the same way about him?

It was time, he reckoned, to formalize the whole relationship. Bring everything out into the open. Clarify matters for both of them.

The prospect of having June as his recognized 'girl-friend' gave him a strange sense of almost boyish excitement, but on the other hand it would be unfair to expect her to continue to visit him in prison week-after-week if she didn't feel in the slightest attracted to him. That could become more of a penance than a pleasure to the girl, if that were the case. And she would probably be too timid to tell him!

The subject had to be addressed!

Short on both the words and the courage to ask her face to face at a visit, Thomas decided to mention the matter in a letter. He was overly anxious to find out if June would ever consider being accepted as his 'girl-friend'.

Written words didn't come any easier than spoken ones, Thomas was soon to discover, but at least he had time, lots of time, to compose them. And to get it right!

It would be simpler to spend time writing a letter than to embarrass the both of them by a stumbling verbal approach, when he would probably end up saying something stupid anyway!

The problem was though, how did you say anything that sounded even remotely sensible in this situation?!

How did you write to a girl and suggest that she become your girl-friend when you still had two and a half years to serve of a prison sentence?

How could you begin to ask a decent hard-working clean-living Christian girl like June Thompson to accept a paramilitary prisoner, albeit a **converted** paramilitary prisoner, as her boy-friend?

Or how could you possibly say to a girl, 'I should very much like us to begin a permanent relationship but the most we will ever see of each other will be half-an-hour every week with a prison officer in attendance'?! That meant, according to a crude calculation Thomas worked out in a contemplative moment, on the back of one of the faithful June's envelopes, that the most they could possibly see of each other would be a total of almost three days in the coming thirty months!

It took him a long time, with many false starts, score-outs, and rephrasings to complete that letter, but eventually he had it finished. And to his own satisfaction.

When he read it over Thomas almost glowed with pride. His letter was as good as he could make it. He had, he reckoned, managed at last to pitch it at the right level. It was warm but not hot, it was sincere but not sickening, and he had, he hoped, succeeded in making his personal feelings for June perfectly plain without presuming to predict hers for him.

Thomas also reached the landmark in that letter which he had been contemplating for some time.

He used the word 'love' at last!

Then, when the letter was posted the waiting began. And it proved, this time around, to be even worse than the will-she-write-back? or won't she-write-back? agony of the first letter of eight months before. Or of the will-you-come-in-here-to-see-me-letter? of February. For now Thomas knew June, and knowing her as he did he was sure that she was the kind of conscientious person who *would* write back. The million-dollar question was, what would she say when she wrote?

For days the love-sick suitor languished.

What was keeping June?

Had she not received his letter?

Or had he overstepped himself in suggesting that they establish a more permanent relationship? Had June not been ready for that, become disgusted, and had thrown the letter in the fire followed by the other dozen or so he had already written?

Was she sitting at that very moment warming her hands at the blaze of his burning letters?

The suspense was unbearable.

Thomas thought a lot, and prayed even more

Every time he thought of June, which was almost all the time, he prayed for her. And for a positive response to his propositions.

When he heard a prison officer yell, "Mail!", as they tended to do every day for the daily delivery, Thomas Martin was first up to see if there was anything for him.

And for two days there wasn't.

June was taking her time. This must be what eternity is like, he thought once. The days just drag on and on, with no end in sight.

The relationship is over. It was lovely while it lasted but now it is finished. I am back on my own, but at least I have God, I can always turn to Him for guidance...

All sorts of crazy conclusions crossed his mind.

Then it happened!

Thomas heard the cry of, "Mail!" and walked out, more in resignation than expectation, just to check that there wasn't anything for him.

One of the next shouts was "3-2-6 Martin!"

It was his name and prison number!

Hoping that nobody noticed either his thumping heart or his trembling hand Thomas took the letter from the officer who was hurrying on along the corridor carrying a motley assortment of mail. Each one of those letters would all be welcomed by somebody, but Thomas didn't care much about any of them at that particular moment. He was thrilled with his. One glance at the handwriting on the envelope told him who it was from. He recognized it instantly.

June had replied, at long last!

Then he was faced with the dilemma of where to go to open it. He wanted to read this very special letter at a very special time. Standing in the middle of a busy corridor with prisoners passing backwards and forwards and his workmates waiting for him on the shift, was hardly the time, or the place.

In a glow of excitement he came to an instant decision. He would hide the letter back in his cell and then open it later on in the evening when he was alone, and would not be disturbed. So that was what he did, and then spent the remainder of the day wondering what was in it!

Question one had been answered in full. June had thought enough of him to reply to his letter. That was reassuring for a start.

Question two was all that remained. What had been her response to his suggestions?

Lock-up was at half-past eight and when Thomas found himself alone in his cell he made a cup of tea and sat staring at the letter which he had placed in a position of prominence. Plonk in the middle of the table it lay, unopened. Thomas was tempted to open it, then he decided against it. He would wait until after the news headlines on his little transistor radio at nine o'clock. The night would be long enough after that, especially if June had said "No!"

At ten past nine he tore the envelope open, as carefully as he could. It would be important not to damage the contents in any way!

Instinct told him to look at the last page first.

How had June signed herself?

'With lots of love' would be lovely. 'Yours faithfully' would be fatal.

What a thrill was awaiting him there!

June had closed her letter, half-way down the final page with, 'All my love, June'. And the rest of the page was covered with XOXOXOXOX! From the middle to the bottom! Kiss, hug, kiss, hug, kiss, hug, in every available space!

Thomas didn't know whether to laugh or cry. He couldn't decide whether he would rather stand up and shout, sit down and sing, or kneel down and thank God! In the space of the remainder of that night he did all of them! Most of them more than once too!

June confessed in her letter that she loved him as much as he loved her. And that she would be delighted to be his girl-friend. The fact that he was in prison didn't matter to her, she assured him. She loved him for who he was, no matter where he was, and she would be quite happy to wait for him until his release, in more than two years time.

Thomas read that letter over and over about twenty times. He wanted to savour the loving sentiment of every sentence. Weigh the loving wealth of every word.

Why should he bother wasting time lying in his bunk, asleep?

It was great! God, and life, and June were all wonderful!

And how he rejoiced!

Now he had a Heavenly Father Who had saved him, and given him peace.

He had an earthly father who cared for him, and gave him confidence.

And he had a girl-friend who loved him, and gave him hope.

Things were looking up!

26

RIGHT ALL ALONG,
AFTER ALL

"Oooops! Sorry, boys!" a freely-perspiring prisoner tendered a cynical and insincere apology as he retrieved the ball from the middle of a Bible study group.

It was a Sunday evening and Thomas, David and four other Christian prisoners were spending their recreation time out in the yard, not playing football as they would occasionally do on other evenings, but studying the Bible. Having chosen the quietest corner of the exercise yard as their base they had hoped to be free from interruption, but that was an altogether vain aspiration. They weren't.

The frequency with which the ball landed in the middle of their group, not to mention the number of other times in banged one of them on the head, led the members of the little group to believe, quite rightly, that the ball hadn't just bounced over there by chance. It had been kicked directly at them, as a provocation. This repeated disturbance was designed to test their tolerance. And it did. To the limit!

Being a Christian in the Maze was no easy option. To stand up for your faith, and to *stay* standing up for your faith, in that environment, required a sturdy spiritual backbone. It separated 'the sheep from the goats' And 'the wheat from the chaff'.

Even the most blatant non-believers had a certain standard which they expected these 'Bible-bashing religious fanatics' to live up to. So for the Christians there could be no compromise with their former pursuits. There could be no truck with tobacco. No peddling in porn. No trafficking in drugs, or anything else for that matter. You were either for Christ, or against Him. Halfway measures didn't exist. Lukewarm, half-hearted, non-committed professing Christians couldn't, and didn't, survive.

The prison regime was a culture of confrontation. If you didn't agree with somebody you told him so, and fought him for it, if needs be. So Thomas and his group of regular Bible readers were subject to all sorts of taunts. They were labelled 'Holy Joes' or 'The Chosen Few', and were jeered at for carrying their Bibles, but perhaps the most difficult of all to endure without an instant and angry reaction was the deliberate aggravation of a flying football up the side of the ear, kicked with enough force to make you 'see stars' for a moment.

Every taunt, every gibe, every crack with the ball or 'accidental' elbow in the ribs was calculated to goad the members of the minority Christian community in the Maze into a violent reaction. To see if they could be provoked into blasphemy. Or propelled into profanity. Made to forfeit their faith and return to their former pursuits.

A few weaker individuals succumbed to such relentless ridicule, but for the most part the Christians in the prison grew in number, in spiritual strength, and in confident witness.

What their persecutors didn't know, or if they did know, chose to ignore, was that this small group of believers had God on their side. And if God was for them, who could be against them?

During those difficult years of witness in prison Thomas Martin drew his comfort from a number of sources. The first two were his unswerving faith in an unfailing God and his blossoming friendship with June. There were other encouragements, too, however, and one of these was the letters from Jean Graham, of Ballymoney, in County Antrim.

The story of Thomas and his conversion in the Maze had been relayed to Jean, who engaged in a very special and singular ministry of writing to people in prison, both with messages of challenge to unbelievers and of support and inspiration to Christians.

These letters from Ballymoney, though not as good for the heart as those from Ballinderry, were always welcomed, for they invariably contained a refreshing spring of sustenance for the sagging soul. They also proved to be beneficial in another way, too, for they gave Thomas some soul-and-scripture searching to do to frame an appropriate reply. So keen was he to delve into the hitherto-undiscovered-by-him depths of Bible truth, and to share it with others, many of his replies to Jean's letters looked more like sermon outlines! Whatever he and his friends had been discussing in their frequent gatherings, Jean received in a letter, plus numerous explanatory and expository asides from the rapidly maturing prison theologian!

Jean often told Thomas, in succeeding letters, of the blessing that his letters had been to her!

One of the greatest thrills that Thomas experienced during those years in prison, after his conversion, was the privilege of sharing the Gospel message, and the faith which he had found, with others.

Despite the endless opposition from a bitter band of godless men, a number of people in the prison, both fellow-prisoners and prison officers often came to Thomas, individually, obviously seeking spiritual help. Many of them had been convicted inwardly, but didn't dare confess it outwardly, by the consistent and persistent testimony of the small but active Christian group in the prison..

On more than one occasion he had men come up to him and instigate a conversation with an approach like, "You are saved, aren't you?"

When Thomas affirmed, "Yes, I am. Do you want me to tell you about it?" the questioner would then continue with a remark like, "My father, or mother, or sister, or girl-friend got saved just last week. He or she seems to be very happy. Tell me, would you, just what does this 'being saved' mean?"

What an opportunity! And Thomas never missed the chance to point a genuinely seeking soul to the Saviour, in Whom he had found such satisfaction.

One such prison officer showed a sincere and enduring interest in what Thomas had to tell him on a number of occasions when they talked.

It had been the officer who had come to Thomas initially, enquiring about 'what had made such a tremendous change in his life', and they had talked repeatedly. Every time they chatted there always seemed to be another question about God, or the Bible, or salvation, or what happened after salvation, for Thomas to answer. And every time, patiently, painstakingly, he answered it.

Eventually the officer made his feelings known to this Christian prisoner, whose now-transparent life and eagerly-acquired Bible knowledge he had grown to respect.

"Thomas," he confessed openly, and bluntly, "I would like to be saved."

Recognizing that this man was in earnest, Thomas invited the officer to step into his cell for a moment. Careful to leave the door open, so that no-one could accuse either of them of any kind of malpractice, Thomas then asked the officer if he would like to kneel down and pray, asking the Lord to forgive his sins, and come into his life as Saviour.

The officer did kneel down at the prisoner's bed, but his prayer was not as complicated as Thomas had tried to explain to him. He had difficulty remembering all that stuff, and perhaps he was scared of being discovered on his knees at a prisoner's bedside, so he just called out Peter's panic prayer with as much urgency as the disappearing disciple had done on the sea of Galilee.

"Lord, save me!" he pleaded.

And the answer came immediately. The response of the Lord was exactly the same as it had been to Peter. He saved the seeking, sinking, supplicating soul.

That night that prison officer 'went on his way rejoicing'. He seemed so happy as he left Thomas's cell to return to other more mundane matters. Now he was, like the prisoner he had just been speaking to, a free man in Christ, a child of God, on his way to heaven.

Late that night Thomas couldn't sleep.

He was turning over in his mind the events of the day. Then he thought of another prison officer he had read about in the Bible, at a place called Philippi. In that incident a prison officer had been saved after observing the behaviour of two other prisoners who had been flogged and thrown into the security cell.

For days to come he reflected upon what God had done, and was doing, in his life.

Eventually, he came to the conclusion that his experience had been very much the same as one of those prisoners in Philippi, Paul. Much later, and a prisoner again himself, awaiting trial in Rome before the unstable and unscrupulous Emperor Nero, Paul described his own situation, when writing to the church which he had seen established in Philippi, despite all the difficulties, thus:-

'I would like you to understand, brethren, that the things which happened unto me have fallen out rather unto the furtherance of the gospel;

So that my bonds for Christ are manifest in Caesar's court, and to all others;

And many of the brethren in the Lord, waxing confident by my bonds, are much more bold to speak the word without fear...'

Since coming into prison Thomas Martin had been saved. He had seen his brother saved. Just recently he had witnessed a prison officer crying out for salvation. Brother David and he had by then placed a tract in every single cell in the prison and were well on their way to doing every cell a second time!

'Rather unto the furtherance of the gospel'... 'brethren waxing confident in my bonds'... 'much more bold to speak the word without fear...'

It was almost uncanny to note how 'the things' which Paul described as having 'happened unto him', had almost the same result as 'the things' which Thomas could recount as having 'happened unto him'.

Each one of those phrases described exactly what had happened, and was still happening, in his life.

A slow, sad smile often crossed his face as he thought back to his father, and what he had had forecast, five years or more before.

And how angry he had been at the time.

'Rubbish!' the recently-imprisoned son had yelled. 'What nonsense!'

'It will all work out for the best you will see!' father had predicted.

'I believe the Lord has a purpose in you coming in here', he had claimed.

The man had been right all along, after all.

27

'HOPE UNITED'!

Just before Christmas 1986, Thomas Martin was informed that he was to be granted his first parole in four weeks time. In mid-January, 1987. On first hearing this heart-stopping news his first thought was for 'Dave'. Has he been given his parole, too? he wondered.

A quick trip across to his brother's cell confirmed the good news. He was to be paroled at the same time.

It was almost too good to be true! After over five years 'inside' they were both going to be allowed to scent the sweet air of freedom again, even though it would only be for two days.

An indescribable sense of eager expectation filled his every waking thought for those four weeks. All sorts of questions chased each other madly in and out through his mind, like playful kittens chasing each other in and out through, and up and down over, the furniture.

What would it be like to be able to walk wherever you wanted, whenever you wanted, again?

Would he still remember all the places, and all the people, he had once known?

Would his former friends have changed, not only in appearance, but also in attitude? What would they think of him, now that he had renounced his old ways, and received Christ?

And what would it be like to spend as much time as he liked with June? Not just half-an-hour at a time, once a week?

It all sounded so fantastic. There were times too when it seemed almost frightening.

Prison was a separate, but also a secure, community. For the past five years Thomas had been conditioned to living with a restricted number of people, all of them adult males, in a supervised society. How would he cope when he was free to associate at will with the general length, breadth, and depth of the general public?

That prospect worried him a bit, at first, but gradually the super thoughts smothered the scary ones, and by the time the last week before his parole date came, Thomas was counting the hours to his release. He was up early, smiling and singing every morning, and he worked with a will all day.

Every hour that passed pleasantly was another hour ticked off towards that magic moment!

When Tommy Martin heard that his 'two boys', as he still insisted in calling the two grown men, were to be allowed home for two days in January he was overjoyed. This, for him, was yet another answer to prayer. He had just one simple request to make, however.

'See if you could get out over a Tuesday night,' he asked. 'Then you could join us in Hope United.'

In an attempt to meet their faithful father's simple request Thomas and David applied for a Monday and Tuesday parole and it was approved, without question. They were to be released at 10.00 a.m. on a Monday morning, and were expected to report back to the prison at 10.00 a.m. on the Wednesday.

When the Monday morning of that first parole came, Thomas was up and dressed long before anyone else was even awake. He hadn't slept much for many nights, and that night he had barely closed an eye at all.

There was so much to think about, to pray about, and to plan for!

At ten o'clock precisely he and David were driven out to the main gates of the prison in a blacked out van. It seemed so strange even to be in a vehicle again!

When they climbed out of the van the two brothers noticed that the guards on the gate were preparing to open up to let them out. A tingle shot up Thomas's spine.

So this was it! At last!

After five years and more of incarceration, and four weeks of anticipation, they were about to walk out of lock-up into liberty, for the very first time.

Thomas and David walked out past the guards at the gate who greeted them with a cheery, "All the best, boys!" and then they were out!

They didn't have to wait long, or look around much to discover a familiar face, however, for there, standing in the car park, all wrapped up against the winter cold, was a man who had longed for this moment almost as much as they had.

It was, of course, their father.

One by one he hugged 'the two boys'.

Tears flowed, but not a lot was said.

For what was there, after all, to say?

This was a moment of wonderment without words. A special period of spiritual communication that could have been spoiled by inappropriate conversation.

When they had completed their initial hearty greetings Tommy Martin directed his two sons to the car he had engaged to take them home. He had asked a friend if he wouldn't mind 'giving the boys a lift'?

As he sat in the back seat of that car on the way back to Lurgan, Thomas gazed in awe at everyday objects. It was as though he had just had the bandages removed after a cataract operation, and had been enabled to see again for the first time in years.

Trees with their stark leafless arms pointing up to the leaden winter sky, bare fields stretching off into the murky distance, cars in new designs he didn't even recognize, were all like Wonders of the World to him.

He felt as though he was a child again.

It felt as though he was learning to live again.

His feelings were precisely those that William Wordsworth described in his 'Ode, ... Recollections from Early Childhood'.

'There was a time when meadow, grove, and stream,
The earth, and every common sight,
   To me did seem
   Apparelled in celestial light,
The glory and the freshness of a dream.'

The freshness of a dream. That was it! It was all a dream! When was he going to wake up and find himself back behind bars?

It didn't turn out to be a dream, though. But every new sight was a new experience. And soon they had returned to 15 Trasna Way, Lurgan.

For almost an hour after they entered the house neither Thomas nor David could sit down. They walked around restlessly, peering into every room, poking into every thing. Some things hadn't changed, they soon discovered, but other things had.

It was the basic furniture that was the same as ever, old-fashioned and familiar, and for the still-edgy homecomers instant recognition inspired immediate reassurance.

Any changes that Thomas and David found in their once well-known home surroundings were in the added extras. The non-essentials. The trimmings. A few new ornaments had appeared. The wallpaper had been changed in two of the rooms. There were a few more gadgets in the kitchen.

When they had finished their eager game of 'I-Spy-With-My-Little Eye' Thomas and David were ready to sit down, and to talk to their father.

Now the embarrassing reticence of the prison gate had gone. And the conversation flowed, interspersed frequently by exclamations from their father which alternated between, "Praise God!" and "I just can hardly believe it!"

That afternoon, when they thought their father could do with a break, Thomas and David went out on their own. Just walking and walking and walking! It was such a novelty to be able to walk about anywhere, and stop to marvel at anything, without the sense of being watched all the time.

The different shapes and sizes and colours of shop fronts, and the different sorts and sizes and prices of goods in shop windows affected Thomas in the same way as the road edges and field hedges had done on their short journey into town in the car.

It was marvellous just to be able to see such simple things again!

Then that evening, after she had finished work, June came round to 15 Trasna Way. Another first for Thomas. And another unforgettable experience! Just to be with the one he had grown to love, and who had kept writing increasingly-warm and increasingly-loving things to him for almost a year now.

What a joy! To be able to spend the whole evening together! Brilliant!

It was almost midnight when June left for home, but Thomas and brother David weren't ready for bed yet! No way! They went out again together and walked for miles around the sleeping town in the biting blackness of a winter night!

They were free!

What was the point in lying in bed?

They were allowed to do that in the Maze, but in there they couldn't just go where they liked, whenever they liked.

It would be time enough to go to bed on Wednesday!

On Tuesday night Thomas and David were the special guests at Hope United, a support group for alcoholics, which Tommy Martin and some friends carried on in Lurgan. After he had become a Christian, Tommy had been concerned for some of his former drinking partners, and involvement in this group was one way in which he thought he could help them.

A capacity crowd attended that meeting that evening for the news had spread like wildfire that Tom and Davy Martin were 'going to be there, and were going to say something'.

Many of those who had followed the fortunes of the two men in prison, but were not members of Hope United, turned up. Brother

Colin was there, with his girlfriend. Florence Cobb, who had been initially, but indirectly, involved in the Tom-meets-June evolving love story was there.

And of course, the two main people in Thomas's life were up sitting near the front, both of them radiant, but for slightly different reasons!

Father, who had arranged the meeting, and who was so thankful to God for how He had answered his passionate prayers, sat silently, expectant.

Beside him sat the girl whom he had come to know and like, because Thomas had come to know and love, June. She too sat silently, expectant, secretly wondering what sort of things Thomas was going to say. Would she learn something about him that she didn't already know? And would he mention her? She hoped not for that would be SO embarrassing!

For over an hour that audience sat spell-bound as first Thomas, and then David Martin told of their experiences. Of life in prison, of their salvation, of the work-party, of the Bible studies. It was interesting and instructive, but above all it was challenging.

If God could transform the life of 'the Martins' could He not do the same for those alcoholics and others who had come along out of curiosity to hear what they had to say?

Of course He could. And 'the boys' told them so. With total sincerity and absolute certainty.

After the hugging and hand-shaking and well-wishing at the end of the meeting were all over, the night had only begun. A crowd of the family and friends returned to Tommy Martin's house where they remained talking well into the night, and when they had all left Thomas and David were 'on a high', and still wide awake.

So they set out for another hike around the town!

On Wednesday morning two suddenly tiring, but supremely happy young men were driven back to the Maze Prison. Although they were going back in again, they could always look forward to being back out again, for their parole period had begun. And they had a memory bank bulging with marvellous memories!

Thomas knew that as soon as they were back in amongst the other prisoners they would have to give an account of all that had happened. He used to love prisoners returning from parole and describing life out beyond the wire, and he was sure that David and he would not be spared that interrogation.

As they walked back up to the gates to be readmitted, that thought must have crossed his brother's mind too, for David turned to him and asked, "What do we do first, Tom, when we get back in here?"

Thomas looked across at him and replied with a weary grin, "You can do what you like, Dave, but I am going to my bed!"

28

OUT OF THE MAZE

For a year after that first parole Thomas Martin anticipated his final release from prison. Further paroles, which had increased both in length, and in frequency, had whetted his appetite for the life of freedom.

Getting out on parole was great.

Going back behind bars was ghastly.

There was a day coming when he would eventually be free. For good.

And he had been promised that Wednesday, 27th January, 1988, would be that day.

How he counted down the months. And then the days.

When would it ever come to hours, he wondered?

It did, though, like things have a habit of doing, come round to that in the end.

The night before that long-awaited ultimate release reminded Thomas of the night before his first parole. There was the same sleeplessness, the same planning of who he would meet first, and what he would say to them. The same adrenalin-charged sense of nervous anticipation.

It struck him like a smack on the jaw, sometime in the early hours of the morning, that he now had a problem, not posed by parole.

How was he going to say his final farewells, his last good-byes, to all these guys around him? Fellows who had been his 'family' for years. What would he say to the boys from the Bible-study group? Or his workmates from the Chief Officer's painting-and-polishing party? Not to mention the prison officers themselves, some of whom he had come to know quite well?

When morning came, it all worked out.

Thomas stepped out of his cell for the last time, clutching the black polythene bag containing all his earthly possessions.

Many of the men to whom he wondered how he would ever say good-bye, were waiting in the corridor. Some of them lounged leisurely at their cell doors. Thomas was going somewhere that morning. They weren't.

One by one they shook hands with 'Tom'.

And genuinely, one by one, they wished him 'all the best'.

The Christians from the Bible-study group found it hardest to see him go. 'Tom' Martin had been a guiding-light in their group for more than four years. They had all grown-up together in grace and in a very practical knowledge of the power of God.

Now he was leaving them. To start a 'new life' outside.

He would never be back. They were going to miss him immensely.

And told him so.

"God bless you Tom!" one choked-up study-member mumbled, echoing the sincerely-felt sentiments of them all. "May God richly bless you!"

With all those good wishes ringing in his ears, Thomas gradually reached the door, from where he was transported by blacked-out van to the outer gate in the perimeter fence.

He was on his way.

It was such an emotionally mixed-up feeling.

In a strange, indescribable way, he felt sorry. Not sorry to be heading out of the Maze, but sorry for the friends and friendships he was leaving behind.

His euphoric sense of inexpressible joy, however, soon stifled that strange indescribable sense of somehow regret.

From now on there would be no more restrictions. No more lock-up. No more long lonely nights. He could see friends, go to meetings, walk up streets, or down them, wherever, and whenever he wanted. And for ever.

Best of all he was going to see June, and then they could develop their plans for their future together, together. The pair of them must have mentioned this momentous moment a million times!

As they had done on this first parole, just over a year before, the prison officers on the gate called a hearty, "All the best Tom!"

He was out of the Maze. Free at last! Released!

As he strode resolutely away from the wire, Thomas never once looked back. It was as though he wanted to instantly forget what lay behind and stretch out immediately to what lay ahead.

The pain was behind. The pleasure was before.

Tommy Martin was waiting for his son, as he had always been, with a car and a driver, in the car park.

Tears of relief flowed freely as a careworn Christian father hugged his grateful Christian son. All the pent-up tensions, the repressed stresses, of the previous six-and-a-bit difficult years suddenly poured forth. It was as though someone had opened the flood gates of some mighty dam and millions of gallons of whirling white water had come tumbling out.

They stood there motionless for all of five minutes. Savouring the moment. So this was it.

The moment Thomas Martin had hoped for, and often thought that he would never see.

The moment that Tommy Martin had longed for, and often prayed that he would live to see.

This was it.

When they had recovered their composure, and Thomas had tossed his black bag into the boot of the car, they set off for Lurgan. Yet again.

On the way home in the car, amidst all the excitement of a

permanent release, Thomas had a question in his mind. It was one that he had toyed with for years, and then months, prior to this decisive day, but he had never been forced to answer.

Now it was staring him in the face, and he had to answer it.

The question was simply, 'What am I going to do with myself now?'

Spiritually he knew what he was going to do. He had taken a decision on that, months before, reading his Bible in his cell. That night he had discovered, in Mark's gospel, the instruction Jesus had given to a man whom he had cured of demon possession.

That instruction was, 'Go home to thy friends, and tell them how great things the Lord hath done for thee, and hath had compassion on thee.'

That night Thomas had made up his mind on one matter. Every opportunity I get, he had determined, I will tell my friends, and anybody else I can, what great things God has done for me. I will testify, anywhere and everywhere I get the chance.

That was good, and his main priority, but the question still remained, 'What do I do with myself, to fill the days, and make money?'

It was a very real consideration, and one over which he had, in his particular situation, little or no control.

He had very little money, and absolutely no influence.

Thomas Martin was, when all was said and done, a convicted, but now converted, loyalist paramilitary prisoner.

God, though, Who had already done great things for him, hadn't finished yet. The truth was, He was really only getting started!

And sitting in that car, Thomas rolled the whole future into His mighty hands.

"Please show me what to do and where to go from here, Lord," he prayed simply. It was all he could do. So he did it. And waited.

Busy, thrilling days of excitement and readjustment followed.

Thomas had come out of prison into a new-to-him community. Before he had gone into 'Crumbling Road' he had moved in an undercover paramilitary activist community. Now his friends were all from the open-and-above-board Christian pacifist community.

What a change. And how they loved him. And wanted to meet him. And hear him speak!

On Sunday, 31st January, his very first Sunday of freedom, Thomas was asked to relate some of his experiences of the transforming and preserving power of God, at the evening service in Lurgan Free Presbyterian Church.

The place was packed that night. The 'bush telegraph' had been busy and people had come from near and far to hear what Thomas and brother David had to say.

For Thomas it was, all in one go, both a humbling and a thrilling experience. It was humbling because who was he that all these people wanted to come to hear him? And it was thrilling because he was being afforded the opportunity to tell all these people about his wonderful Saviour.

At the end of that service nobody seemed to want to go home. Dozens of people crowded around to chat to 'Tom and Davy'. It was all so warm and welcoming.

As the congregation eventually began to disperse, Robert Russell, a church elder, came across to where the two brothers had come together, and were now talking to each other.

After congratulating them on the 'great meeting', Robert went on to pose the question that was on his mind.

"I hope you don't mind me asking," he began, "but have you boys got a job yet? Or would you want one?"

"No, we haven't got jobs yet," Thomas replied, wondering what was afoot. "But we could do with one, I'm sure."

Robert then went on to explain the situation more fully.

"A Christian friend of mine runs a landscape gardening business and is always looking for good staff. If you fellas would be interested I could speak to him for you. Would you be keen on that sort of work?"

"Oh yes, we would," Thomas replied almost instantly, with David nodding in agreement.

What the man didn't know was that these two men would have been glad of the prospect of ANY kind of work, for neither of them had any money. They were both stony broke!

Before the conversation ended it was agreed that Robert would speak to his friend with a view to giving Thomas and David a job in 'a month or so's time', when gardening work was beginning to pick up again after the winter, and after they had been given a chance to settle down and see around.

One of the supreme thrills of being out of the Maze forever, was that Thomas and June, who now realized that they loved each other very much, and wanted to share the remainder of their lives with each other, could start making serious plans for the future.

And one of the first things they did was to go out, in February, and buy an engagement ring! Then they announced that they were hoping to be married in June! When else could June be married?!

All their friends were delighted for them. Wonderful! Marvellous! Exciting! they all exclaimed.

What they didn't know was that Thomas Martin had no money!

What they didn't know was that June had to lend her fiancé the money to buy her the ring, out of her savings!

But the young couple had a lot of things going for them!

They were deeply in love with each other and they were both deeply devoted to God, Who had demonstrated the depth of His love to them by sending his Son to provide eternal salvation for them.

He had provided for them before. And would do so again.

Step number one was that on Tuesday 1st March, 1988, Thomas Martin, with his brother David, began work with Cecil Haffey Landscaping, of Portadown.

What a lot he had to be thankful for!

God had preserved his life and saved his soul.

God had seen him into, through, and out of the Maze.

God had provide him with a kind and caring girl who loved him, and was prepared to marry him.

And now God had provided him with a job, and a permanent source of income, when dozens of discharged prisoners were finding procuring employment a problem!

'Go back and tell them', Jesus had said, 'about the great things the Lord has done for you'.

Thomas had already done that, every time he had been given even half a chance.

And he would do it again, too.

Thousands of times!

29

'ALL THESE THINGS ...'

From Thomas and June decided, while Thomas was still in prison, that they were 'meant for each other' they began to pray for one another. And they had it so arranged that their prayer time would provide a link of love in the chain that was binding them ever closer together.

At ten thirty every evening, June, no matter where she was, and Thomas, who had no other choice to be anywhere other than locked up in his thirteen foot by eight foot cell, spent five minutes praying specifically for each other, and for their plans for the future.

Next only to God, Whom they had both decided should have priority in their lives, Thomas and June meant more to each other than anybody else. So as they asked God to guide them together through the coming days, they had adopted as their theme text, the precept-with-a-promise of Jesus, from the Sermon on the Mount, 'Seek ye first the kingdom of God, and his righteousness; and all these things shall be added unto you.'

Now that Thomas was out of the Maze it was time to put their prayers, and their plans, into practice.

That did not mean, however, that they could stop praying, for they were soon to discover that as the planning began in earnest, it was only then that the praying began in real earnest, too!

In March, 1988, Thomas and June both became members of Lurgan Free Presbyterian Church, and within a week they had asked Rev. David Creane , to conduct their wedding ceremony in the church on Saturday 18th June!

Thomas now had a job, and a regular pay packet, for which he was very grateful both to God and Cecil Haffey. But he was left with a few matters still to resolve.

He and June had arranged to be married on an agreed date, but as yet they had nowhere to live as a married couple. They couldn't make any plans for 'setting up a home', for they didn't have a home to set up!

That, too, although the biggest problem, was only the first one!

What about all the expense of a wedding with all its trappings?

Then there was a honeymoon. What about it? It certainly couldn't be New York. It could perhaps be Newcastle. But it would be more likely to be Nowhere.

Finance was the problem. Thomas who had come out of prison with all his worldly possessions in a black bin-liner, had just begun to work, and although June had been saving hard out of her weekly wage, her name still hadn't appeared on the list of Upper Ballinderry's Top Ten Richest Women.

Where were they ever going to find a home, and pay the rent of it, to start with? And buying a property would be out of the question for a released prisoner with no money.

Then there was the wedding... And the honeymoon... And housefurnishing, of the house which they still didn't have...

"We will put God first in our lives no matter what happens. He has provided for us before and I am sure He will do so again," Thomas declared all bright and breezy and big-brave-man-like to June one evening in early April, when plans, but nothing else, seemed to be advancing.

Secretly though, below all the bravado, his own faith was being severely tested.

Did 'all these things' stretch to houses? Or weddings? Or honeymoons?

Not to mention more mundane matters such as tables and chairs? Cups and saucers? Knives and forks?

Or light bulbs?

The answer to the first and foremost of these questions came just about ten days after Thomas's confident to June, but not quite so clear to himself, predictions of God's provision.

It was after a Church service that Matt and Linda Wylie spoke to Thomas.

"I hope you don't mind us asking," Matt began, and Thomas found his heart skipping a beat. The very last time somebody had begun a conversation with him using those very words he had ended up getting a job out of it!

"But do you and June have anywhere to live after you get married?" was what Matt hoped he wouldn't mind being asked.

Trying to sound ever so matter of fact despite the fact that his heart had just skipped two more beats and had now restarted with the sole intention of hammering its way straight out of his chest, Thomas replied, "No. Not yet. We are still looking for somewhere in Lurgan."

Having established that the soon-to-be-wed couple still had no home to go home to, Linda had a proposal to put to them.

"My father died there some time ago, and his house is still vacant. If you and June would like to use that house, which isn't all that big mind you, you can have it, rent free for at least a year."

Thomas was dumbfounded.

How kind of Matt and Linda! And how good of God!

"Thank you very much!" he was almost tongue-tied in an attempt to express his gratitude. "That will be wonderful. We will certainly take you up on your offer!"

Then as he was moving away, Linda said softly, "And there's something else, too, Thomas. I would like to give June my wedding dress, if that would be all right."

Now he was totally speechless!

God had chosen to use his people to both provide June and he with their first home, and solve the first of their wedding considerations, all in the one conversation!

And there was more!

When it became known amongst the congregation that they were to have a wedding in the Church on June 18th, some of the ladies approached Thomas and June together one evening, again after a service.

"We would just like to say that if you haven't anything arranged yet about a reception, we will put on a meal for you in the Church Hall after the ceremony," they offered. "You won't have to worry about a thing!"

That was great! That would save Thomas worrying about a thing, and the big thing he had to worry about, the big thing he *always* had to worry about these days, was, "Who's going to pay for this?"

So he asked.

"And what about all the expense of it?" he enquired. "What you are talking about will cost a good bit of money."

"We said not to worry about a thing," one of the ladies reiterated. "So don't. We can come to an arrangement about that which will suit you, later."

Then there was the honeymoon. What about it?

When he looked at his financial situation, Thomas concluded that it would take a miracle for them to have a honeymoon. So God provided one.

Some friends from the Faith Mission approached Thomas independently, and without any prior consultation with each other, with the query, "We heard you were getting married, Thomas. Have you anything sorted out about a honeymoon?"

When the reply to each question was invariably, 'No, not yet' the suggestion to come back was exactly the same. "You ought to try the Faith Mission College in Edinburgh. They have special rates for young Christian couples."

That was fair enough, but who did Thomas Martin know in The Faith Mission College, Edinburgh? All of the Christians he knew, up until the last three months, except his father and his wife-to-be, were in Her Majesty's Prison, Maze.

There was a solution to that problem, too, though. For one of the ladies who had made such a suggestion went one step further. "If you like, I will make enquiries about it," she volunteered. "And if it is free on your dates I will book it for you."

A few days later she came back with the news that they could have their honeymoon in the Faith Mission College, Edinburgh, for seventy pounds for the both of them for ten days. The price she hoped wouldn't be too expensive.

Too expensive! By no means.

It gave Thomas something to set his saving sights upon. He thought he could just about scrape up seventy pounds before the 'big day'.

When that 'big day', the long-awaited wedding day, came, it was wonderful. So many friends turned up at Lurgan Free Presbyterian Church to convey their sincere best wishes to the young couple, and Rev. Creane and his congregation were there almost to a man. And the women who had kindly offered to 'put on a meal' exceeded all of Thomas and June's most imaginative expectations.

The wedding and the reception were so happy and relaxed, and such a crowning blessing to the young couple who had begun their tentative 'penpal' relationship three and a half years before.

They spent their honeymoon in Edinburgh as planned, and on their arrival home to their rent-free home, they discovered that someone had been busy when they had been away. The whole house had been redecorated. From top to bottom.

Little did they know but when they were away on honeymoon, humbly thankful to God for all his goodness, a work-party had descended upon their house to have it totally repainted and substantially refurnished for their return.

They were completely overwhelmed. It was unbelievable!

God had provided everything for them.

'All these things' had indeed meant everything they had needed.

They, hadn't had to 'worry about a thing' as the good lady had said.

Their wedding reception had been marvellous, costing 'a donation towards the price of the food'. They had just returned from a wonderfully happy honeymoon, at minimal cost. £3.50 each per night, full board!

Now they had arrived back into their rent-free first home to find it completely equipped for comfortable living! Everything they needed was there!

The tables and chairs. The cups and saucers. The knives and forks.

Even the light bulbs.

And it also contained many luxuries that Thomas had only ever dared dream about during his years 'inside'. Many of these had come in the form of wedding-presents from well-wishing Christian people from all sorts of places!

Linda had described the house as being 'not all that big, mind you', but Thomas was delighted with it. To him it was something like a palace! It was certainly a lot bigger than his thirteen by eight cell, and that had been the de luxe accommodation. It had been even more cramped 'on the protest'.

When the last of their 'just-called-round-to-welcome-you-home' guests had gone, Thomas and June sank down tearfully on to their knees at their new settee.

'All these things' had been 'added unto them'.

Thomas said, 'I think we should make that the motto for our new home, June.'

"What do you mean, Thomas? Is it 'seek ye first the kingdom of God' you are talking about?" June was puzzled.

"Yes, you know we have always tried to live by that verse, and still will do," her new husband went on to explain. "But that's not what I am talking about now."

Then turning her head round gently, but firmly, as though it was attached to some mechanical toy, he said, "Read that."

And June duly read the words which were embroidered across a new firescreen they had been given as a wedding present. They were the words of Joshua's affirmation and declaration in the Bible, when he had announced boldly, 'As for me and my house, we will serve the Lord'.

'O.K. Thomas I agree with you," June concurred. Then for emphasis and to hear how it sounded, she read aloud their new watchword.

'As for me and my house, we will serve the Lord.'

Thomas and June pledged themselves, there and then, that their new home would be a place in which they would 'serve the Lord'.

How could they do anything else since the Lord had 'added all things unto' them?

Had he not given them their home and everything in it, in the first place?

And above all He had given them each other.

What choice did they have, but to serve Him?

30

I WANT TO GO NOW

It was strange.

Thomas and David Martin considered peculiar.

The father who had supported them so valiantly during their imprisonment, seemed to lose all interest in life, and living, soon after they were released.

This was totally contrary to their expectations for they had imagined that their freedom and ability to see him and be with him at will would have granted him a new lease of life. But completely the opposite occurred.

What his 'boys' were inclined to forget was that their father was now beginning to look, and feel, his age, with their period in prison having contributed at least in measure to that ageing process. An indomitable spirit had kept him going over the past seven years, surmounting all sorts of obstacles, to support them in prison.

Now physical weakness, and spiritual completeness, had taken over.

It sounded to those who knew him that he considered his course complete. His mission accomplished.

All three of his sons visited him regularly, and on one occasion, when fighting for breath with his asthma, he panted to Thomas, "Son, I just want to get home." Although he was at home, in 15 Trasna Way, Thomas understood perfectly what he meant.

His father wanted to leave the trials of this world behind, and set off for heaven, his ultimate, eternal home.

Later that evening, as Thomas drove back to his heaven-sent earthly home in Lurgan, that statement of his father's rolled over in his mind. And it twanged a string of recollection.

There was a story, somewhere in the Bible, that described a similar situation.

What was it?

Thomas tried to think.

The first one that sprang to mind was Paul's signing off letter to Timothy when he could claim confidently that he had 'fought a good fight, he had finished his course, and he had kept the faith'. Those things were every one of them true of his father. He had fought an uphill battle, he had kept **the** faith with God, and steadfast faith with his sons, and now he obviously considered his course complete.

That was good, and appropriate, but it wasn't the story Thomas wanted. They were very similar in sentiment, the stories. There must be a link somewhere...

So Thomas began to repeat to himself the words from Paul's second letter to Timothy, as he remembered them...

'I am now ready to be offered, and the time of my departure is at hand.

I have fought a...'

Then it dawned on him. The link was there.

It was in the departure.

Paul had been sitting in the departure lounge, waiting to board. For the final leg of his journey. And so, too, had this other man.

Of course, it was Simeon.

Luke's description of the scene was graphic. An old man in an ornate temple holding aloft a tiny baby and proclaiming,

'Lord, now lettest thou thy servant depart in peace, according to thy word : For mine eyes have seen thy salvation.'

How true that was. And how it so perfectly portrayed his father's present position. Both in attitude and ambition.

In the same way that the ageing Simeon had been so content to depart, because he had fulfilled a lifelong ambition, to see the baby Jesus, 'the Lord's Christ', so the ageing Tommy now appeared content to depart, for he had also fulfilled a lifelong ambition. To see Thomas and David saved. And safely out of the Maze.

In two years Tommy Martin's health deteriorated steadily.

When 'the boys' came home, in early 1988. Tommy Martin was making monthly visits to the doctor's surgery with his asthma.

By the end of the year he was seeing the doctor almost every week. Even the slightest exertion left him battling for breath.

Late in 1989, the ailing father contracted pneumonia and was hospitalized for some weeks. Although he was allowed home for a period after that, he was by now too weak to do anything. Or go anywhere,.

All he ever wanted to do, his only and utmost aim, was to 'go home', to heaven. And soon.

Then, in February, 1990, he took pneumonia again.

His three sons, for whom he had sacrificed so much, took it in turns to sit by his bedside in Craigavon Hospital. He had given his life to support them, and now they were forced to sit helplessly by and watch the life ebb slowly from his embattled body. A body which years of early drinking and latterly bouts of debilitating asthma, had left in a sorry state.

As Thomas took his turn to sit with his father, and heard him gasp for breath, he often thought of happier, and sometimes sadder, days. An occasional and involuntary tear would well up in his eyes, as he recalled the night he had told them that he had something to tell them... the morning when he thought the police had made one mighty mistake when they had hustled David and he from the house...the day he had sat in the gallery of Crumlin Road Courthouse to hear them sentenced...and then more than six years of weekly visitation.

Often, later, as he gazed on the form which was lapsing in and out of consciousness, and listened to the rhythmic, hollow, snore-thump breathing in the oxygen mask, Thomas recalled those visits. Those years on the Yamaha step-through.

There was the day when he had come in, absolutely drenched.

"What happened you father?" Thomas had asked, alarmed.

"Oh, it was a big lorry, son. The road was flooded and the lorry went through it and soaked me!" had been father's light-hearted explanation.

Then there was the day he had come in, with frost crystals sparkling on his eyebrows and the stubble of his beard. He had looked more like 'Jack Frost' than Tommy Martin, that day.

"You shouldn't have come, dad," had been his son's instinctive reaction.

"I just had to come, son," had been father's immediate response.

The worst of all had probably been the day when father had gone into The Maze to visit his 'boys', with what had patently been a dose of 'flu. He had been shivering uncontrollably and trying unsuccessfully to wipe the globules of cold sweat from his forehead, without anyone noticing.

Thomas had been really worried that day.

"You shouldn't have come, dad," had been his distressed reaction.

"I just had to come, son," had been his father's deliberate response.

The long days, and even longer nights, of waiting and watching were soon to come to an end. The battling for breath was soon to be over.

On Sunday, 25th February, 1990, the body of Tommy Martin gave up the struggle to survive, and permitted the soul of Tommy Martin to do what it had wanted to do for months, possibly years. To go now. And to go 'home'.

Simeon had prayed, 'Lord, now let your servant depart in peace; for mine eyes have seen thy salvation'.

Tommy Martin had been granted both those desires.

He had departed, in peace.

And in a very real way his eyes had seen God's salvation.

31

DON'T WORRY, I'M COMING TOO!

During those spring days of 1988, those planning-a-future-with-more-faith-than-finance days, Thomas and June, now firmly committed as-husband-and-wife-to be, attended the Easter Convention in the Martyrs Memorial Free Presbyterian Church, in Belfast.

It was a thrill for Thomas to see so many Christians gathered in one large building to study the Bible. What a change from four or five, or on a big night nine, huddled together in the corner of an exercise yard or crammed into a tiny cell!

The high-point of the Convention for both Thomas and June came on Good Friday night, 1st April, when Dr. Brian Green from London was the speaker.

A capacity congregation listened enraptured as he challenged them as to the character and compass of their Christian witness, choosing as his text the words from Philippians chapter one, 'For to me to live is Christ, and to die is gain.'

The entire thrust of his message was the necessity of giving oneself wholly and unreservedly, 'as a living sacrifice', unto God.

At the close of the service an appeal was made for anyone who wanted to dedicate their lives to the Lord to come forward.

Thomas sat motionless for a few minutes, his head bowed, and his hands over his face. Tears began to trickle through his fingers. He was weeping, and he had reached an emotional position when he didn't care who saw him weeping.

In prison, to weep was a sign of weakness.

In church, to weep was a sign of brokenness.

Then, rising slowly to his feet, he looked down at the back of the hat on the bowed head of June. She, too, must have been touched. He leaned forward and whispered into her ear, "June, I am going up to the front."

Raising her red-eyed face to look up into his red-eyed face, June half-smiled as she whispered back, "And so am I!"

Together they made their way up to the front of the church and while the congregation sang, Thomas and June knelt down and dedicated their lives to the service of God.

During the next week, though, when they were both back at their daytime jobs, they wondered how they could fulfil their vow most completely? And serve the Lord most effectively?

That question began to be answered as Thomas was having his own period of personal Bible reading, some days later. When reading in the Old Testament, Thomas was arrested by five words from the instruction God gave to Joshua, after the death of Moses, in relation to the leading of His people into the Promised Land.

'Arise, go over this Jordan', was the phrase which seemed to shoot off the page at him.

'Arise, go over this Jordan'. What could that mean?

After pondering the matter for some time, the only conclusion that Thomas could come to was that he should perhaps pursue the proposition which some folks had suggested to him, but which he, up until then, had dismissed as impossible because of perceived problems up ahead.

He should enter the Whitefield College Of The Bible and train for the Christian ministry.

Although Thomas had dedicated himself both willingly and wholeheartedly to God, he had never once considered himself a possible candidate for a College.

How could a recently-released paramilitary prisoner, with no formal education or qualification, and only a minimal amount of money, ever hope to met the entrance requirements of a Bible College? Or pay the fees, if by some sort of miracle he should be accepted?

Good idea, but not possible, he decided, and tried to banish the entire notion from his mind.

That, however, didn't prove possible, either.

The words kept boomeranging back at him.

'Arise, go over this Jordan.'

And he kept bouncing back to Joshua chapter one.

It was another two weeks later, and during yet another excursion into that story that Thomas was pulled up short by the question at the beginning of the ninth verse.

'Have not I commanded thee?' it asked, but it came across to Thomas more as an accusation than a question.

It hit him with a bang.

'I have told you to do this. But what have you done about it?'

Then he read the verse over in its entirety, repeatedly...

'Have not I commanded thee? Be strong and of a good courage; be not afraid, neither be thou dismayed: for the Lord thy God is with thee whithersoever thou goest.'

That verse seemed to render all his real-to-him reasons for not considering Bible College as an option, null and void. It cut his excuses to pieces.

The promise of the Lord's abiding presence could see him through all his fears for the future. No matter where Thomas went, or what obstacles he was called upon to encounter, he was not going to be asked to go anywhere, or do anything, alone, or in his own strength.

"Don't worry," the Lord had assured him, "wherever you go, I'm coming too!"

Although this was still prior to their planned wedding, Thomas shared his thoughts with June, after this second, and as he saw it, emphatic, revelation.

His soon-to-be-bride agreed with him that God was directing him towards Bible College, and she wondered if she should join him there, so that they could both prepare for Christian work.

After the elation and commotion of the wedding, the honeymoon and the settling in to live in Lurgan had all subsided, she decided against it, however.

Just as clearly as God had directed Thomas to set his sights on Bible College through the story of Joshua, so from that very same narrative God showed June that he had another role for her to fill. Reading one day in Deuteronomy chapter three she discovered verses which she had never known were in the Bible before.

'Thou shalt not go over this Jordan,' she read in verse twenty-seven. 'That is clear enough, anyway,' she thought.

Then, reading on, she found out what she was expected to do. God had something, no less important, for her as well.

'But charge thou Joshua, and encourage him, and strengthen him: for he shall go over before this people...'

Her place was not to be in Bible College. It would be her duty to support her husband. To strengthen and encourage him. And also, more practically, to continue in her job to help buy food. And clothes. And books.

Although Thomas was now convinced that he should pursue a course of study in the Whitefield College of the Bible, he discovered, upon making a number of enquires, that the entry requirement to the College was at least three 'O' levels. And he had never sat an 'O' level in his life!

How was he ever going to meet the stated admission criteria?

It seemed a daunting task, but the Lord had told him to be neither afraid nor dismayed. He had a job for Thomas to do, and He had promised to see him through.

Where there's a will there's a way, or so they say.

Early in 1989 the prospective student did two things. Firstly, he changed his job and began working as a fitter with UPVC Windows, and then he also enrolled for night classes, to study English Language.

Having never undertaken any serious study of this nature before, and having a full-time daytime job, and a new wife at home, Thomas decided to gain the necessary 'O' Levels, a year at a time, if he could.

English Language this year. English Literature the next year. And, if he lasted that long, History in the third year!

Although it was going to take him at least three years to prepare himself for Bible College, for the formal and in-depth training for Christian service, Thomas didn't waste those three years as far as his pledge to serve God with all of his being for all of the time was concerned.

Word soon spread amongst Free Presbyterian churches about 'this chap who was saved in prison and has a tremendous testimony' and soon Thomas-with-the-tremendous-testimony was telling it all over Northern Ireland!

When not away in Ballymena or Ballymoney or Ballyroney or Ballysomewhereelse, Thomas witnessed to everybody who would listen to him, workmates, neighbours, family and friends. And all his leisure time, which ten years previously would have been spent in pubs or paramilitary parties, was spent in tract distribution and door-to-door evangelism.

Then came the good news. Having met the stipulated standards, Thomas Martin was offered a place at The Whitefield College of the Bible.

He was to commence his studies in September, 1993.

From the moment he first crossed the threshold, Thomas loved life at College. The opportunity for intensive Bible study was wonderful, and Thomas particularly relished the teachers and the teaching. In prison he had ample opportunity for individual Bible searching, but had never experienced direct and systematic Bible teaching. The times of fellowship with Christians of like mind as himself, too, were a special treat, and he found himself able, on a number of occasions, to act as mediator and arbitrator between fellow-students. He had never even dreamt of it at the time, but life in prison had been preparing him for that.

There was just one matter that concerned him for a few weeks at the commencement of the first term. It was to do with the old problem. Finance.

To a certain extent, Thomas had entered the College on faith. He reckoned that by the end of the year he and June would probably have saved up enough to pay his fees.

The humiliating bit, the moment he was dreading, was having to tell the College authorities of his situation.

And the miraculous bit came when he approached them, apologetically, to explain that he hoped to be able to meet his expenses, 'sometime before the end of the year'.

"Don't worry another thing about that, Thomas," he had been told. "Your fees have already been paid!"

"What do you mean?" the first-year student had retorted, flabbergasted. "I haven't given you anything yet!"

"That's right, we know that," they had agreed. "But an anonymous donor has paid your fees for all of this year. Now you go on and enjoy the course!"

What a discovery! And what a proof of the Lord's promise. And provision.

The Lord had assured Thomas, from His Word, that He would be with him, and would provide for him. Wherever he went. And that must include into Bible College. So why should he worry? About fees or anything else.

Having his fees taken care of, by an anonymous well-wisher, was only the start of God's practical provision for His humble servant during his studies.

Someone else provided him with all the books he needed and an occasional envelope, slipped unobtrusively to him after a meeting with a whispered, "Here you are, brother, that's for you!" helped meet his travelling expenses from home to College.

Then on 17th August, 1994, when Thomas had just completed his first year of study, he and June had their first happy taste of parenthood. Their little son, Aaron, was born. What a joyful, thrilling, uniting experience that was for them!

Perhaps the biggest test of their faith to date, and the most practical proof of God's provision for a young couple determined to serve Him, came more than a year later, just before Christmas, 1995.

Thomas and June both knew the problem.

They had spent all the money they had in preparing a very modest Christmas for themselves and their little sixteen-month old son. But they had nothing left, nothing whatsoever to buy any Christmas presents for anybody else.

It was so embarrassing. Family members from both sides, and a whole galaxy of friends, had been coming and going for days showering them with kindness, and they couldn't afford to give them anything in return!

Thomas said to June one night, as they were perplexed about this matter, "June we will have to lay this before the Lord. He will see us through!"

So they did. Day by day, and night by night. Christmas, though, was fast approaching and the people were still arriving on their doorstep with still more goodies. But still they could not afford to return their kindness in any way!

Christmas Day was on a Monday that year, and up until Friday night, December 22nd, they had prayed earnestly, but with apparently no response.

And although trying to appear outwardly calm, inwardly they were both beginning to panic.

There was only one more shopping day left until Christmas!

They were both in bed, just before midnight, when they heard a rattle at their letter box, and then the sound of a car being driven away. When Thomas made his way into the hall he found an envelope lying there on which were written the words, 'To Thomas, June and Aaron. May God bless you at Christmas.'

When he opened that envelope, with trembling hands, Thomas found that it contained three hundred and fifty pounds, in cash.

From an anonymous donor.

So tomorrow they could buy presents for all!

The young parents were astounded, again!

For God had not only provided enough to cover their present list , but there turned out to be enough left from that gift to run their car until the end of January as well!

Not only had the Lord kept his promise to be with them, He occasionally took a few steps ahead of them, too!

32

JUST THE MAN FOR THE JOB

The early months of 1997 brought both increased pleasure and a certain creeping sense of uncertainty to Thomas and June.

Their pleasure came with the birth of their second son, Samuel, in February. As well as allowing Thomas to glow once more with parental pride Samuel's birth afforded him the added amusement of telling his fellow students that he now had a scriptural family. For 'a certain man had two sons'!

And it was the fact that Thomas was fast approaching the end of his course in College that gave June and he that sense of uncertainty. That wondering about the future.

There could be no doubt but that God had more than kept His promises to go with them, so far. And had provided for their every need, so far. But now they needed Him to go before them, again. And show them His will for them, again.

Whatever were they going to do, or wherever were they going to go, when Thomas had completed his College course? And now they had two little sons to provide for as well.

There was always that worry.

God, though, had gone before. As He had done before...

During the last two years of his College course, Thomas had spent one day every week serving the Lord in a practical capacity, engaged in visitation work amongst the congregation of Lisburn Free Presbyterian Church.

So, as he approached the summer of 1997, when he was set to say Good-bye to the relative security of student days for good, Dr. John Douglas, Principal of the Whitefield College of The Bible, and also minister of the Church in which he had been doing his placement visitation, approached Thomas with a proposition.

"I was wondering if you would consider helping me, Thomas?" he began. "As you know I am very busy with my work both as Principal here, and also as minister in Lisburn. You have been well accepted by the congregation there, and we in the Church would like you to join us for a year, as my full-time assistant. How would you feel about that?"

Thomas would feel great 'about that'. And told him so. He had already begun to establish a rapport with the congregation in Lisburn, and accepted at once. This was yet another answer to prayer.

A year's full-time ministry. What an opportunity to gain experience in preaching the Gospel, in teaching the Scriptures, and in home and hospital visitation. He couldn't wait to get started.

That proved to be a wonderful year of learning! Thomas had heard someone say once that they had never really learnt to drive the car until they found themselves behind the wheel on their own, one day. It was the same in that year. Thomas Martin began to experience for himself both the delights, and the difficulties, of the Christian ministry. Although under the guidance of a mature and caring senior minister, Thomas began to discover what it felt like to be 'behind the wheel on his own'.

As the end of his one year term loomed up ahead, however, the concerns for the future began to creep in again.

They weren't allowed to linger for long this time, though.

It was after an early morning prayer meeting one Tuesday in the summer of 1998 that Dr. Douglas invited Thomas to 'take a seat there for I want to have a chat with you'.

What was coming now? What was this all about? Had some other church 'called' him? Was he going to have to leave Lisburn?

Thomas felt a bit funny. Had he not made the grade as a minister? Was he about to be...? Well, what?

He needn't have worried, however. What Dr. Douglas wanted to 'have a chat with' him about turned out to be very simple, yet very satisfying.

"The session of the Church here have decided to invite you to become my co-pastor in the work. We have all been impressed with your ability and willingness in all aspects of our work in the past year, and we would like you to contemplate joining us here on a more permanent basis. Under the proposal we wish to put to you, I would be retained as senior minister and you would become my co-pastor, taking responsibility for much of the day-to-day running of the church," was the message he had been asked to convey to the somewhat stunned Thomas.

The last few words of what Dr. Douglas had been saying seemed to float off into oblivion on a cloud of fancy, far away.

The younger man was thrilled. Absolutely delighted.

Here he was, being offered a permanent position.

His mind raced.

Off the streets and into The Maze... Out of sin and into salvation... Out of the Maze and into work... Out of work and into Bible College... Out of Bible College and into the Christian ministry...

'How good is the God we adore...'

Suddenly he was arrested from his reverie. Dr. Douglas was still speaking.

"We would like you to give this matter some serious consideration, Thomas," was what he was saying. "You will have a month to make up your mind. Think about it and pray about it, and then let us know your decision."

A month! To make up his mind!

Thomas wouldn't need a month. Or a week. Or a day. Or even an hour!

He could have given them his answer there and then. But didn't. He refrained.

It would probably be best to 'pray about it'. And anyway, it would be good to let June have her say.

In less than three weeks Thomas told his senior minister what he could easily have told him that marvellous Tuesday morning. He had decided to accept the session's invitation. Subject to the approval of the congregation he would willingly become co-pastor of Lisburn Free Presbyterian Church.

Obtaining the approval of the congregation proved to be no problem. They had grown to love and respect Thomas during the years he had already worked amongst them. A meeting of the entire congregation was arranged, at which they unanimously accepted him as their minister.

All that remained now was for him to be ordained into the ministry of that Church. And that was going to be some experience...

The date for the 'Ordination and Installation of Mr. Thomas Martin as co-pastor of Lisburn Free Presbyterian Church' was arranged for Monday, 7th December, 1998.

Thomas felt strangely excited that Monday morning when he woke up. His mind kept flitting back to his first parole. The sense of the unexpected. The questioning of his ability to cope with what he was about to embark upon. The oh-so-new-ness. The what-am-I-going-to-do?-ness.

When it came almost time to set out, June and he took turns at dashing to the mirror. She to see how she looked in her new outfit. And Thomas to see how he looked in his new collar. This was the first time he had even worn a clerical collar and he felt all choked up in the thing.

There was one consolation about the collar, though. It helped him to allay his fears of earlier in the day. His friends back in Lisburn must have thought that he could preach like a minister, and teach like a minister, for now they were actually permitting him to LOOK like a minister!

Thomas felt extremely nervous as he and June started off to drive from their home in Lurgan to the church in Lisburn.

This was a big, Big, BIG night.

All his relations had been invited to his ordination service, and most had promised to come. And ninety-nine per cent of them were not Christians. What would they think of it all?

Dr. Ian Paisley, Moderator of the Free Presbyterian Church was going to be there, too. And would be taking part in the service.

Suddenly, just as though he had been struck by lightning, Thomas was besieged by all sorts of doubts. And fears. And misgivings.

'What sort of a minister are you going to make?' the devil began to cast up. 'A member of the U.V.F. A non-conforming paramilitary prisoner a preacher?! Now that's a laugh...'

As he drove along that road that night, to what he had thought was going to be one of the biggest nights of his life, Thomas's whole past life came up before him. In glorious technicolour.

Sweat broke round his new clerical collar.

He wanted to rip it off and throw it out the window.

Thomas Martin was seriously contemplating turning around and going back home, when two things happened. Almost simultaneously.

In panic Thomas had begun to pray. Driving along, with eyes open and mind awhirl he had begun to use, as a plea from the heart, David's prayer from Psalm twenty-five, 'Remember not the sins of my youth, nor my transgressions: according to thy mercy remember thou me for thy goodness sake, O Lord.'

He had just started to repeat the first seven words of the verse over and over again to himself, 'Remember not the sins of my youth, remember not the sins of my youth, remember not the...' when something else happened.

The lights of the car picked out a sign on the side of the road.

'H.M.P. Maze', it said.

It was there for a moment. Then it was gone.

They were away on. Past it. On their way to Lisburn.

And suddenly there was a great calm.

The storm was over.

The mind was at rest.

That was it!

The past was gone. It was behind him. It was forgiven.

His former life in Lurgan, and his many months in the Maze were all history now. And he was driving ahead, driving forward, to a new life, and a new challenge. In Lisburn.

As Thomas took his seat at the front of the Church that evening and looked down upon a sea of faces, he was humbled. All these people had come to see him ordained as a church minister.

They were there from all arts and parts, and in all capacities.

He spotted some of the wide representation of relatives. Many of them were wondering what to expect. Some of them looked slightly edgy. But at least they had come...

There seemed to be a crowd of men in clerical collars. Ministers from other churches all over the country had come along to pray God's blessing upon this newest addition to their ranks.

Dozens of his friends from Lurgan who had supported him so practically after his release from prison, the ravens who had brought the bread in a time of famine, had all travelled down to Lisburn.. There they were, dotted all over the church, smiling up.

Then there was David. He was there. They had been through so much together.

And June. The girl-friend who had stayed loyal, and was now his wife, and the mother of his two sons...

When it came Dr. Paisley's turn to speak he took as his text some words from Ezekiel chapter twenty-two, verse thirty. 'And I sought for a man among them,'. He then went on to describe how God was looking for men. Special men, with special talents, to serve him in special situations. Just the man for the job.

When Dr. Paisley had finished Rev. Thomas Martin, the newly ordained co-pastor of Lisburn Free Presbyterian Church, stepped forward to speak. And he simply gave his testimony...

A soft hush fell over the packed congregation as Thomas told of his former life in Lurgan, of his father and his conversion, of the U.V.F., of The Maze, of the night he was saved, of witness in the prison, of his release from prison, his wedding, his call to Christian service, Bible College, and now this... His voice began to tremble as he told them that he was the first person ever, from such a background, to be ordained to the ministry of the Free Presbyterian Church.

As he brought his testimony to a close, nobody in that vast audience, however, had any doubt about the new minister's suitability for the post. With just such a background he was ideally equipped to deal with any soul in any situation. From the Moderator of the Church down to the most unchurched relative they were all ready to agree that God had found His man.

And had brought him out of the Maze to place him into full-time Christian ministry.

Just the man for the job.

AMBASSADOR

Belfast Northern Ireland Greenville South Carolina

OTHER BOOKS BY THE SAME AUTHOR

MY FATHER'S HAND

THIS IS FOR REAL

JUST THE WAY I AM

SOME PARTY IN HEAVEN

FIRST CITIZEN SMYTH

SOMETHING WORTH LIVING FOR

HOW SWEET THE SOUND

AS OUR HEADS ARE BOWED

ONLY THE BEST WILL DO

A BRUISED REED

BACK FROM THE BRINK

THE TANGLED LAMB